# Pocket Full of Pie

Thomas Clay Jr.

BookLocker
Saint Petersburg, Florida

Copyright © 2020 Thomas Clay Jr.

ISBN: 978-1-64718-108-6

All rights reserved. No part of this publication may be reproduced, stored in a retrieval system, or transmitted in any form or by any means, electronic, mechanical, recording or otherwise, without the prior written permission of the author.

Published by BookLocker.com, Inc., St. Petersburg, Florida.

Printed on acid-free paper.

BookLocker.com, Inc.
2020

First Edition

Library of Congress Cataloging in Publication Data
Clay Jr., Thomas
Pocket Full of Pie by Thomas Clay Jr.
Library of Congress Control Number: 2019920019

This book is dedicated to Wendy Braff.

I was in a very bad situation living in Austin Texas when I got a friend request from Wendy. We became fast friends and before I knew it she came to Austin to see if I was as great as Satan himself. That said a lot about her but when she volunteered to sit in line for three hours to get some Franklin's smoked brisket, I knew she was a contender for the best human being ever.

Before I knew it, she invited me to live in the heart of darkness where some dreams come true but nightmares begin. Being exposed to the full spectrum of debauchery in Hollywood has been quite an education for this Kentucky boy. I still resist the urge to become a homeopathic vegan yoga instructor with a side business in healing crystals but it may become too overwhelming at some point.

Wendy took a lot of disorganized and unedited stories of mine and turned them into this book and I am eternally grateful to her for seeing something in me that many did not. If you're fantastically lucky in life, you'll get to call someone like her your friend.

Thomas

I'd also like to thank Ruth and Arnold Braff for their generous support, and my Kickstarter donors, especially Suzanne Parker, Magelyn Jay Stewart Willborn, and Joy Moss.

Thomas

# Table of Contents

| | |
|---|---|
| Meadowmark | 7 |
| Dr. Morasutti | 16 |
| My Old Kentucky Home | 24 |
| Tyrone | 30 |
| James Clay | 33 |
| Mom's Cancer | 41 |
| Dolly | 45 |
| Trouble | 50 |
| 11 Minutes | 56 |
| Albrecht Durer | 63 |
| Gary | 67 |
| Judy | 73 |
| Lance | 82 |
| Lyssa | 91 |
| Mr. Randall | 101 |
| War | 105 |
| Dean | 116 |
| Shania Twain | 119 |
| Nicole | 136 |
| Rachmaninoff | 141 |
| Best Drugs Ever | 144 |
| Pop's Toolbox | 148 |
| Spain | 151 |
| Ted | 156 |
| Mrs. Theiss | 159 |

| | |
|---|---:|
| Atticus Finch | 164 |
| Brother Tim | 172 |
| David | 181 |
| Donnie | 184 |
| I.Q. | 188 |
| Jail Tale | 192 |
| Ron | 198 |
| Jeopardy | 203 |
| Lesli | 208 |
| Mary | 211 |
| Maybe | 216 |
| Mrs. Whitney | 218 |
| Peregrines | 222 |
| Monsters Among Us | 224 |

## Meadowmark

You have to have a certain kind of mind to put your finger on something that's hard to understand. This isn't easy for me to talk about either because it forces me to look back on my youth when I was as ignorant as I could be. I was very much a product of my southern White Anglo-Saxon Protestant upbringing.

The first black person I ever saw was when we were on our way to Danville. I was four years old and we stopped for gas, and I saw this old black man walking in. I followed him in and asked if I could touch him. He put his arm down and I asked, 'does it wash off?' He had a deep bass voice that sounded like a rumble, "Oh no, Son. It don't wash off."

That was 1974 and that man must have been in his 70s or 80s. He had thin, wrinkly skin and deep crevasses in his face. He was wearing dark blue bib overalls. I can hardly fathom what that man had seen in his life. He saw an Agrarian society switch to an industrial society. The first road and automobiles.

The first airplanes. Two world wars, jet airplanes. And more horror and depravity from the era of Jim Crow.

I wonder what he made of a little white boy asking him that.

Danville, Kentucky is a railroad town where the poor white trash was on one side of the viaduct and the rich people lived in town. It's a very beautiful place, actually. Centre college is there, where it churns out the children who will soon become the bourbon gentry.

There was an old country store about two blocks from my grandparent's house. Pop kept a coffee can full of pennies and when we were kids, we'd get the pennies and go get some candy. There were about 20 jars full of candy. The root beer candy canes were my favorite. They were a nickel. There was an RC cola bottling plant less than a mile away, so they were just a quarter.

Garnet lived just across the street and he had some blue tick Coonhounds that he would sell for over $1,000 each and this was in the 70s. He shipped them to the Philippines, strangely enough. If you've ever heard the commercial for Purnell's Old Folk's country sausage, the man in that video sounded exactly like Garnet. Garnet always smelled like tobacco because he chewed this stuff that came in a yellow package. My great grandmother also liked it. It was disgusting. One day my uncle Chuck came over drunk -as he always was- and sat down next to Garnet.

Chuck was just a hateful man. He hated everything. He couldn't get anything to ever work. Pliers and remote controls seemed to give him the biggest fits. He was my Pop's brother. Pop never took a drink. He was in 7th grade when he had to quit school and take care of everyone. Chuck, on the other hand, collected Nazi flags, a couple of Rugers and a few Hitler youth knives he took off of Germans he killed in the Battle of the Bulge. He was the opposite of my Pop. So, Chuck is piss drunk and Garnet is sitting there on the cinderblock wall and Chuck picks up Garnet's RC Cola spit bottle and takes a big swig of it. You've never heard such a commotion when he started puking it back up. We nearly pissed ourselves laughing.

Uncle Chuck landed in Normandy on D-Day. He fought in the Battle of the Bulge. He had slick red hair that he put tons of Brylcreem in. He got shot a couple of times and stayed in the Army until those "goddamn Commies took Berlin." Chuck was a real son of a bitch and a mean drunk. I knew to avoid him. Pop only had one eye, so the Army rejected him. Pop told me: "he was never right in the head when he got back."

I had already raided the penny jar and was bound to get my RC cola and some candy canes. The store was only a block from Garnet's house, so he came with us. I walk in and if you've ever been in a country store, you know that heavenly smell it makes. Like biscuits and candy all mixed together with old wood. I am eyeing the candy selection as I am gnawing on a Bit-O-Honey when I hear a big ruckus in the back.

"GET THE GODDAMN HELL OUT OF HERE! Get out before I sick the dogs on ye!"

It sounded like a stampede running from the back to the front door. Four black kids go sprinting out. Mary was the old woman tending the store. She lived upstairs. She had a sweet southern accent.

"Oh Garnet they just keeds."

"Mary, you cain't let these little N-words in heah!"

"They ain't done nothing but get them some pop and candy like these heah."

*Pocket Full of Pie*

When you're a kid, you don't know when you're being poisoned, that's just the way it was. My Pop was as poor as those kids and he was just as ignorant as Garnet was. Pop got kicked by a mule when he was just a kid, that's why he was blind in that one eye. He would 'slick up' some bikes and give them to the kids, the black kids. People would bring him their old bikes to fix up for the kids. Garnet would come in and say: "Ed, why you wasting your time fixing up them bikes for them little monkeys?" He'd leave in disgust. Whenever pop wanted me to listen, he'd put his arm on my shoulder and lean in so only I heard him.

"I wasn't nothing once just like them kids. They cain't hep it that they's poor."

Then he'd pull away and say, "You never know son, one of them might grow up to be Meadowmark Lemon."

When Pop was a cab driver, the Harlem Globetrotters came through and broke down. He took them to the only hotel in Danville. This was in the early sixties. The guy at the front desk told Pop he couldn't let them stay.

"What's the trouble?"

"We don't let N-words stay here Ed. Take 'em to Lexington.'

So he did.

They were in two station wagons. Cousin Arnie was driving the other cab. No hotels in Lexington either for the same reason. The two white guys with them got rooms after making a spirited protest. The alternator had gone out on their bus. Pop couldn't pronounce Meadowlark so he was Meadowmark. His 'main man' Curly was 'poison with a basketball, son.'

Meadowlark said, "Well boys, it looks like we're sleeping on the bus." It was snowing bad by then.

My granny was a seamstress and her mother did nothing but quilt. So bedding was never an issue at their house. "Oh no son," Pop said. "Y'all gonna have to stay with me and Gerl." Geraldine was my granny.

"Oh no sir, we couldn't do that."

"It just wouldn't be Christian of me to let you fellas freeze to death out heah."

It was already past supper when Pop brought in the biggest men Granny ever saw. She had the best fried chicken there was in Danville ready and a mess of biscuits and gravy when they pulled in. She had just been to the Piggly Wiggly and she fired up the skillets and proceeded to feed these men.

That night they were laid out on the floor and Lawd hab mercy, you never heard a ruckus like these fellas snoring.

Granny woke up at 5 am her entire life. So she went back to the Piggly Wiggly to get some more bacon for breakfast. 5 pounds of bacon, fried taters, eggs, toast and coffee were her standard breakfast.

Pop went by to get an alternator that would work on their bus and put it on for them. At this point in the story that I heard at least a thousand times, Pop would put his arm around me and say, "And that's when Meadowmark pulled out his billfold and laid five $20 bills on me." That was big money to Pop. They came back a few years later when they were passing through just to have some of Granny's cooking again.

There was a poor black kid from Akron who grew up to be something. He's been married to the same woman. He has beautiful kids and he built a school for the poor black kids just like he used to be. He bought them uniforms, shoes and bikes so they can get to this beautiful school he built for them. Some people call him LeBron. Others call him King James. This is what Donald Trump said about him:

"Lebron James was just interviewed by the dumbest man on television, Don Lemon. He made Lebron look smart, which isn't easy to do. I like Mike!"

Dehumanizing people is the vulgarest tool every debased ignorant racist has used to inject their vile poison into the consciousness of any other dull-minded simpleton who is dumb enough to think they are better than Don Lemon or LeBron James. The difference is that the President is supposed to be the best of us.

Trump defiles everything we are as a country and he is teaching children that it's okay to dehumanize the very best of us because of the color of their skin. He has debased every noble notion that has made our country great. But what is most disgusting about this menace to society is that he is telling black children that two exemplary men they look up to are not worthy of praise, even when they are celebrating opening a new school for kids just like them.

The damage that racist imbecile does is incalculable.

When he is gone, the collective sigh of relief will echo off of Jupiter.

## Dr. Morasutti

My dad guarded nuclear weapons in Germany during Vietnam. I was born there. When his tour was over, one of his friends was an artillery commander and as a farewell present, he gave dad an artillery projectile to use as a paperweight.

This projectile was peculiarly heavy. It looked like a large bullet, but it was solid metal. I used to play with my sister Cathy when we were children and I'd put it between my eyes like a bullet like Yosemite Sam would do. So did she. One day, Cathy dropped it on her foot, and it swelled up terribly and it turned black. When dad got home, mom said, "Tee get that goddamn thing out of my house!" It was made of depleted uranium. No, he didn't know.

I started having headaches when I was 13. It was just unrelenting pressure in my left eye. My dad was a Major in the Army then and boys did not whine about headaches.

At first, they might happen every couple of months. As I got older, they were more and more frequent. They completely wiped me out. I used to run five miles in the morning and five miles after school. It helped with the pain because I was swimming in endorphins a lot.

When I was 19, this one night I had the worst headache I'd ever felt. I was on all fours and ramming my head into the wall. My mom had cancer at the time. She came in and asked me what I was doing. I told her I was trying to stop the pain. So she went in her room and brought me a hydrocodone pill. It was the first time I ever had narcotics. About 20 minutes later, the pain started to lift. It was as if something unclogged my brain.

As I wrote my English papers after that I knew something was weird. Then a few days later I couldn't play chess. I was making mistakes a novice would make. I could remember everything before like a camcorder in my brain. Now it was all jumbled as if my index had gone haywire.

Ten years later my pain doctor looked at one of my MRIs and he saw four calcifications in my right hemisphere. He asked me if I remember one headache being worse than the others? I knew instantly which headache he was talking about. I told him that I used to remember what happened on one particular day of the week and was a master chess player but after that headache, I couldn't play chess anymore and my filing system was all jumbled.

"Well that's because you had four strokes."

I had two MRIs in '91 and '94 read by the same Radiologist that missed my very large brain tumor. He wasn't a Neuroradiologist, so he missed it. Twice.

My family tormented me for a decade for taking 'those damn pills.' My dad most of all. I was 29 when I saw a Dateline NBC that saved my life. I knew I had the same tumor this guy on Dateline had. I had seen 27 specialists by then and most told me it was because I was depressed or that it was all in my head.

When the blood test came back, my prolactin factor was 38,000. I delighted in telling my sisters and my dad that it was a brain tumor.

I can't really tell you what it is like to visit a Neurosurgeon. The first one who saw me looked at my name and said he couldn't help me because my dad is a famous lawyer in Kentucky and this doctor had just been relieved of several million dollars in a malpractice case and he wanted nothing to do with me.

The first time I went to see Dr. Morasutti, I was with my dad and by some miracle, I had saved the 91 MRIs. It was just the initial consultation. The Neurosurgeon lifted that one out first and put it on his light board which was outside his office. Dr. Morasutti popped in and innocently asked, "why didn't you get this out in 1991?" He didn't know what he had said.

My dad looked at me like a dad who loved his namesake, and his head turned beet red. I knew when that happened to flee, except this time he wasn't mad at me. He goes, "excuse me." I saw him outside on his cell phone pointing in the air like he was commanding artillery batteries as he did. The window was barely cracked and I could hear him: "and this stupid motherfucker malpracticed on my son TWICE! You get Mikell and Bill on this right now because I want that bastard's ass on fire by the end of the week!" Within minutes I had all the lawyers I knew what to do with.

In just a few seconds, all the misery I had been through for 17 years became relief. It was the first time I felt like my dad was on my side and not my adversary.

When we had our settlement conference, Dad insisted it happen at his office which was on the top floor of this building in Louisville. It was very impressive to look at, but I heard dad tell Mikell: "hell no, I want to look that bastard in the eye." The funny thing was that the Radiologist got three of his classmates down as expert witnesses. We had his professor as ours. When Mikell met with him, she handed him my '91 MRIs and he said: "are you going to give me any of the symptoms?" She goes, "headaches."

He put them up on a light board and said, "oh geez, he has a huge tumor on his pituitary gland and it's growing around his optic nerve."

Mikell goes, "is this something that a competent Radiologist could miss?"

"Anyone who missed this would flunk out of medical school, and if he somehow did make it through, they should have their license to practice medicine revoked."

Dr. Morasutti ordered a fresh MRI so he could plan the surgery. The next time I came to his office, I was in his waiting room for three and a half hours and I was really pissed off. So they rescheduled me, and I left strict instructions that if he was going to be that late again to respect my time, goddamnit. By some weird happenstance, I was watching the Discovery Health channel and they showed the exact procedure that he was planning for me. It was gruesome. They go up the roof of your mouth through your nose and peel a good part of your face up. Then he goes into the base of your skull and take a hammer and chisel and cut a square hole right next to your carotid artery and vein. The surgeon was giving commentary as he worked and said: "you have to be careful here because one nick and the patient will bleed out."

I really did not want to go through this because my mom had cancer and I saw doctors fuck up all the time. The next time I went in to see Dr. Morasutti, I was good and mad about the last visit and this time I waited an hour and a half. He's Canadian and was known nationally for his stance on tort reform. I was sitting there wagging my foot ready to give him a piece of my mind. So finally we get called back and it was another 30-minute wait.

"I'm really sorry about the wait but some things take more time than you think." All that hot air dissipated immediately. I was picking a man that was going to use a hammer and chisel next to my carotid fucking artery and by god this fucker better know his shit! So I started asking him what he studied in college. Quantum Physics and Evolutionary Biology. I know a bit about that, so we started talking about that. I didn't know he knew what I was doing, but he did. It was two hours before we even started talking about the procedure.

It takes more confidence than you or I can imagine to crack someone's skull open and start working on their brain. In my mind, I was resigned to death. I didn't care because I just wanted to stop the pain. I had sharpened a spoon once on a grinder until it was razor sharp so I could gouge my eyes out. My family just called me a whiny bitch that complained about headaches. My mom was the only one who never abused me. I really only wanted to ask him one question and it took me 3 hours to ask him with the gravitas that I wanted. I was scared out of my wits, believe me.

Dr. Morasutti had a very calm voice. "You're not going to slip up with that hammer and chisel work, are you?" I asked him point blank. He looked at me like he was talking to his Maker: "I've never had a problem with it before and I do know what I'm doing, Thomas." He did not waver at all. It was absolute confidence. I wasn't resigned to death anymore. I thought I might live through it. It was 18.5 hours of surgery. He wore Crocs. They were hideous. I told him, too. "For my kind of job, they do wonders."

I was on an extreme amount of narcotics then. The night before the surgery, my wife was down in the dumps. She put on a brave face. We made love like it was the last time. I couldn't sleep. As they were taking me back into the operating room, I said to her: "I'm sorry I'm putting you through this."

"Love is not love which alters when it alteration finds."

She was so beautiful. I wish she were alive so I could remind her how much it meant to me.

## My Old Kentucky Home

The Kentucky Derby kicks off every year with Thunder over Louisville. They set off over a million dollars in fireworks. They have the Chow Wagon which is a bunch of really fatty overpriced fair food. It's both disgusting and awesome.

Spring in Kentucky is among the best things there is. The smell of all the flowers, cut grass, the myriad of flowers that were planted on the roadways decades ago when the public would spend money on such things. Derby week is grand in so many ways. The airport is teaming with private jets from all over the world. The hotels are so full, people rent out their extra rooms for $1,000 a week. Most Kentuckians are duty bound to do nothing on Derby Day.

Except the poor ones, of course.

Some people have made billions off of the human misery of Kentuckians, myself included. They're the ones flying in Gulf Streams and Leer jets to see what their unbridled greed has bought them. They never get to see that part of course, by design. Those in charge know not to let the old moneyed jetsetters see the human squalor that Kentucky meticulously conceals during the big show. Hell, the hardest working people in Kentucky the month before the Derby are Kentucky's prisoners who have been cleaning up the garbage for a $1 a day.

I can only imagine what it must be like for the profiteers from Oxycontin. Staring down from Millionaire's Row at Churchill Downs at all the pomp and circumstance splayed out below on the bluegrass as they raise their Juleps skyward to toast the greatest country in the world, knowing not only did they make billions from enslaving their fellow man to chemicals, but profiting off the many industries that prosper from their incarceration. Hunter called these reprobates 'the bourbon gentry' because that sounds a lot more charitable than describing them for the grendels that they are.

There's something corrupting about the limestone and horse shit in Kentucky that seeps down into the marrow of anyone who has spent any amount of time there. Mark Twain famously said of my old Kentucky home: "When the end of the world comes, I want to be in Kentucky because it's always twenty years behind the times."

Native son Hunter S Thompson memorialized some of the debauchery that occurs on the first Saturday in May in his famous essay: 'The Kentucky Derby is Decadent and Depraved'. It was, is, and will forever be exactly that. Every two-bit hustler and hooker trying to make a decent living are there every year, but nothing compares to the lowlifes pounding down mint juleps by day and gargling Chateau Lafitte Rothschild by night in the vast array of soirées hosted by the upstanding social elite in the Bluegrass State the last couple of nights before the greatest two minutes in sports.

What I miss is the life before I was consciously aware of how horrific my home state truly is. That's why Kentucky is home to the greatest bourbon and opiate abuse problems in the nation, and everyone else pays for the evil that sits in power. They're the ones clear-cutting the rainforest and saying: "see what I am doing for you? I'm building you a good road for businesses that will create jobs!" Only in Kentucky, it's called mountain-top removal and you can retaliate with: "yeah but you're destroying everything that matters for those jobs."

They'll just ignore you and call you a Liberal as if it is some slight, which it is, if you're as dumb as a stump.

On Derby Day, a hundred thousand people will invade Churchill Downs to witness the greatest horse race in the world. A band will pound out the notes to My Old Kentucky Home which is easily the greatest state song there is. You can't grow up among the stench of horse shit and bluegrass and not tear up when you hear it. I's that beautiful, except when it's not.

'The sun shines bright in the old Kentucky home,

'Tis summer, the darkies are gay;'

Aye, there's the rub. They've changed the words Stephen Foster wrote for his song. 'Darkies' has been changed to 'old folks' to conceal the embarrassing truth that well, slaves were probably not 'gay' about living in bondage. Kentucky being the ever-foresighted place of progressive thought, has been grappling with its state song for quite a while now, along with its apparently terrible miscegenation problem. (wink)

Apparently, a lot of Yankee agitators are unhappy with our venerated observances and old-timey remembrances and want to completely destroy Stephen Foster's state song! Ain't it enough that we have to change the hallowed words to make all the blacks happy? Why, if we keep going, they gonna want reparation checks and they done talking about it now on the Ellen show by gum! That's our heritage! Why should we change our venerated observances for a bunch of uppity interlopers that only come once a year? I ain't changing the words just to suit all them! Or make them comfortable! I'm not letting anyone forget our heritage of slavery, Jim Crow and racism. I'm going to rub it in the faces of every goddamn Grendel on Millionaire's Row until the truth shines bright on my old Kentucky home!

When they play My Old Kentucky Home every derby, I lose it. It is simultaneously the most racist and beautiful state song there is and it's especially apropos because that is what Kentucky is. The racism there is more nuanced than overt, as it is just south but it's still there, marrow deep as it is across the south.

There's something about home that borders maybe on cheap sentimentality when you leave it. I left Kentucky and will never return except under the most extreme duress and I cannot think of anything that would cause me to return. The Derby is a grand show, but it deflects from the reality that

Kentucky is one of, if not the most wholly corrupt state in the union. Everyone, and I mean EVERYONE who administers the abomination they call the judicial system there is corrupt. From the "good cop" that witnesses dirty cops breaking the law and says nothing, to the judges who passively listen to these criminals lie under oath on a daily basis. It's all a façade, as I am sure is true in other states. Nobody that works for such a corrupt system that pays their mortgages is ever going to do anything to change it, especially there.

I don't miss My Old Kentucky Home, not one fucking bit.

## Tyrone

One summer I was at my Pop and Granny's house. Pop just went up to the 7th grade so he never had a proper education. He was good with his hands. He grew up picking nails out of burnt down buildings to work on his farm. We were working on a bike because Pop would pick up the broken bikes and fix them up for the kids in his neighborhood. He knew that poverty was the worst form of violence.

So we come out into the garage and the side window was open and a bunch of pop's tools were gone. It didn't really matter because he had at least two of everything, but he was a bit upset. He never cussed. He was a Christian and the very best of the best of them.

We kept working on this bike for a couple of days. It was a Schwinn with a big skid tire. We painted it candy apple red with a white stripe down it.

A couple of days after the tools went missing, a woman named Juanita brought her son down by the ear to Pop's garage. He was carrying the missing tools. "Tell Mr. Waits what you done, Tyrone," The boy was maybe 13 or 14. He teared up and said: "I'm sorry Mr. Waits. I stole your tools."

Pop went over to him and put his arm around him like he did, and said: "but you brought them back so I forgive you."

We finished the bike a couple of days later. It looked so good. Pop told me to load it up. I drove as he guided me a few blocks away. We get to this house and he gets out and goes up and knocks on the door. 'Nita.' He couldn't say Juanita. 'Bring Tyrone on out here."

Tyrone came out with his head down. Pop put his arm around him again and said, "climb up on the back of old Blue and pull that cover off."

The sheer look of joy on his face is something I can never convey with words. He looked at Pop. "It's yours, son." It was a seminal moment in my life.

As we drove away, I asked, "Why him Popa?"

"Because he needed it the most, son."

At his funeral, a stranger walked up to me and grabbed my hand.

"You don't remember me, do you?"

"Sorry."

"I'm Tyrone. You brought a bike to me."

He had grown up to be a foreman at Caterpillar with four kids. He said: "Your pop changed my life. He was the change in my life."

They called my Pop the King of Beech Street.

Be the change.

## James Clay

My grandfather James Clay was as racist as can be. He disowned my father when he married my mom because she was literally born on the wrong side of the tracks. He was a famous lawyer in his own right. He won a lot of big cases I can hardly remember now.

He had a monster intellect. I didn't meet him until I was 14. He was in a similar pissing contest I have with my dad and I doubt we'll ever run out of piss. He loved bourbon. He was an alcoholic who was full of pride. Those aren't good traits, in case you were wondering. He had to be right about everything and he was never sorry for anything.

We had a lake house on Lake Herrington. My uncle Jimmy wasn't welcome because he and Grandfather Clay got into a pissing contest too, only Jimmy was much more stubborn, supposedly. They fought about something, I don't know what it was, but they practiced law in the same small town for 40 years and never spoke to one another, even though they practiced in the same building. At the lake house, we had a long table that could seat 20 people and when Grandfather Clay spoke everyone got quiet like the king was holding court. He was horribly funny, and guests would often guffaw, pounding their hands on the table.

He was deaf. He wouldn't wear hearing aids. My dad is deaf too but at least he wears hearing aids. I need them too. My hearing loss is from the brain tumor and theirs was from loud stereos. Grandfather loved Jazz. No, you don't really understand. He had every single Jazz record there was. I mean all of them. And he knew the name date and birthdate of every one of the artists. All black. A thousand or more records.

The lake house was a famous watering hole. Pineapple Jims with breakfast - which was country ham and redeye gravy. I didn't like it much because it was so salty. We'd go to the dock and women would drink sangria or some other 'foo foo' drink. There was a boozer in Burgin where everyone would stock up because Danville was a dry county since all the Evangelicals wanted it that way. They drank as much as the Clays would. Bloody Mary's were another favorite. In the 80s, if you didn't spend $500 on booze then you weren't expecting guests and there were always guests.

Grandfather had two girlfriends in his 70s. He waited until his youngest, uncle Ritchie got married before he divorced my grandmother. It was a point of honor (eye roll). We were headed to Burgin once for bait and booze and he says to me and dad: 'when I was a young man, I thought only certain women were beautiful. As got a bit older, a lot more of them looked good. Now at my age, hell, they all look good!'

I used to have this Porsche 928 and I did not drive under 100 mph. Usually 120 on the highway. I was cruising through Anderson county one day on my way to Danville at all of 100 mph and I didn't see the state trooper hiding. He comes screaming out. I know I am stone cold busted. I pulled over fast.

"Do you know how fast you were going?"

First of all, you can't show fear to a State Trooper.

"Well I had the cruise control set at 100, I hope that's accurate."

"You were doing 102 in a 55 mph zone."

"Well that's what I get for trusting a Kraut odometer, trooper."

"License and proof of insurance."

"Yes Sir."

You have to be from the south to understand what 'yes sir' means. Gentleman are raised to say this to their fathers. I did with my dad until I was 14. It shows you were raised right. So the trooper comes back quite quickly.

"Any chance you're kin with James Franklin Clay the attorney?"

"I'm going to visit my grandfather right now. He's sick." (a flagrant and shameless lie but fuck tha police).

"Well there's no sense in me wasting my time writing this ticket out then is there?"

"Nope."

"Tell your granddad Trooper Thomas hopes he feels better."

"Will do."

I spent two days with Grandfather Clay once. By this time, he wasn't practicing law anymore. He first taught me how to tell the difference between good bourbon and paint stripper. He pulled a bottle of Pappy Van Winkle which he bought by the case. He had Maker's Mark and Wild Turkey and a bottle of Dowling. So you put your hand over the bottle top and just get enough to wet your hand and you rub them together until the alcohol is gone and then you smell the mash. The stronger the mash smell, the better the bourbon. Pappy Van Winkle was the best, then the Dowling -which isn't made anymore- then Wild Turkey and then Maker's Mark.

He woke up drinking Pineapple Jims, but an Old Fashion was his preferred cocktail. If I drank, I'd probably drink only those, but I didn't inherit the love-of-alcohol gene most Clays have. Then we listened to Jazz for two days. It didn't really jive with my Van Halen brain, but I was stuck there and decided to learn. By the end, I understood why Charlie Parker, Duke Ellington and Fats Waller were geniuses. He called them geniuses, n-word geniuses. I couldn't reason that. He revered these people. It was the greatest source of joy for him. He employed a black woman for 25 years to be his kids' nanny and cook.

So was he a scoundrel with a few redeeming qualities? Was he a good man whose naked racism came from the environment he was a product of? I never knew him but from those few times I was around him. He was an old drunk to me. His alcoholism was so bad my uncle Ritchie put him in a retirement home. When he dried out, he begged everyone to get him out. Ritchie thought he had dementia. He was just drunk all the time.

When you're a kid, you go along to get along. That's the way it is in the South and for white people now. You see a little racism and you don't say anything. You see Eric Garner choked to death on video by a cop and some demon in your head makes you rationalize murder: "well, he shouldn't have been doing something illegal" or "he shouldn't have resisted." Sometimes you see so much horror that you come to a crisis of conscience about it.

My dad has a very short fuse. He had a client once named Rodney. He was a black guy who kinda liked to 'reappropriate material goods for other uses' that *may* have been purchased by someone else. He was a very affable and funny guy. He was also very good. Well the cops had a boner for him because Dad had beaten several cases they charged him with, until they got him once red-handed. I remember the night he got convicted. Dad was really angry and was slamming Old Fashions. He sat on the couch twisting his feet in a circular motion. He hated losing. This was something he thought he should have won, but the jurors convicted. I heard him on the phone talking to another lawyer and he said: "they convicted him because he was black."

When I moved out of my dad's house, all those chains the rest of my family tried to put in my brain just faded away. At least I thought so. You can't just hope a poison like racism goes away without pulling it out root and branch. Racism's sole function is to dehumanize human beings to justify treating them like shit or worse still, with indifference. Indifference that keeps us from confronting injustice such that Eric Garner and Philando Castillo suffered along with many others who were murdered by the police.

Racism doesn't just rear its ugly head when cops kill an unarmed black American. The worst place in this country that it rears its ugly head is in every courtroom and jury room in this country. If we are in this 'post racial society' as Chief Justice John Roberts put it, why do black defendants get sentenced to almost twice as much prison time as white people do for the exact same crime? There is no other explanation for this "curious phenomena."

In my 48 years on this planet, I've noticed the infirmity of racism is also accompanied by the infirmity of religion and that's why I hate both of them to the core of my being. I've also come to realize that people of color can never cure this scourge no matter how excellent they are. A thousand more Toni Morrisons or Michael Jordans or Oprahs can never fix this affliction.

Some people will have this difficult conversation with themselves and you might not like what you discover about yourself, but change is ever-needed.

## Mom's Cancer

By any reckoning, I should be dead. I've had 4 strokes, a massive brain tumor that took 18.5 hours and two surgeons to remove. I have an aneurism on my carotid vein. I've driven 120 mph in cars for years on end. I took 12 oxycontin 80 milligrams and 10 mg of Xanax all at once trying to stop the pain of life I could no longer bear.

My Mom was 35 when she first learned she had cancer. She had a hysterectomy in 1980. Her surgeon said he got all the cancer out. No need to worry.

It was a cold and rainy Saturday when my sister Cathy came bursting into my room, "Mom has cancer again." I went on autopilot. I leapt from my bed. Threw on some clothes and used all the 400 horsepower my 1970 Buick Riviera could muster to get to her. Nothing else mattered but keeping her alive.

When I got to her room, Dr. Eckerle was there. He told her she had about 3 months at best. "Sorry Patsy."

Mom had a very slow growing ovarian cancer. She told the surgeon/gynecologist who did her surgery that she didn't feel well. But he knew best because he cured her cancer and she was a woman that would do better listening to a man. And he did everything wrong as you can imagine: "There there, Patsy. Now you're just a bit hysterical and you need a mood stabilizer."

What she really needed was an X-ray to show the mass growing in her abdomen that was the size of a grapefruit when he finally got around to taking it out seven years later.

He came in to make rounds. I looked at him with murderous rage, "I guess it wasn't all in her head, was it, asshole!" Everyone at the nurse's station turned to look because I was that loud.

I didn't have to tell her surgeon he was fired. He didn't come on rounds again.

The first thing mom said when he left was, "I want to be buried above ground." I wanted to cry but I knew I had to be the strong one now.

They gave her three months to live on December 2nd, 1987.

She lived 10 years, one month, one week, one day, 14 hours and 42 minutes past that.

My dad cheated on her. You can imagine what that is like for a woman that was captain of the cheerleading squad and who looked like Marilyn Monroe in her prime. My dad would often tell people that there were three full drawers of a filing cabinet in the Oldham County courthouse regarding the Clay v Clay case. They went to court 63 times. I was 19 when I realized that this was not normal. Great love can quickly become the most vengeful and bitter hatred with a simple twist of the fate-knob.

Dad took us to Miami for vacation while mom had surgery. Yeah.

When you first hear your death sentence, you're sad. Then you get mad. When my mother was mad, she was a 5'5" mushroom-cloud laying thermonuclear bomb that would scare a category 5 Hurricane. No, no really. She's in medical textbooks for living longer than anyone else with an undifferentiated metastatic cancer.

At one time, my sister had AML leukemia, mom had ovarian cancer and my Pop had esophageal cancer. They were all doing chemo and radiation on the same ward at the same time.

The worst cruelty of life is that the older you get, the more people you lose, and you'd think that it would get easier. It doesn't. It just gets harder and harder. When I lost Jellybelly, I couldn't have another cat because it hurt so much to lose her. I waited six years to get Squiggles. Far too long, really.

In my Senior annual, I quoted Thoreau because this line meant so much to me in my youth: "Significance changes as do meanings as experience taints your vision." I think that's what Mr. Blake was getting at in Songs of Innocence and Experience. Thoreau said in Walden: "Time is but the stream I go a-fishing in. I drink at it; but while I drink, I see the sandy bottom and detect how shallow it is. Its thin current slides away, but eternity remains."

Nothing in this life is more important than the trail of love and honesty you leave behind. Ugliness and cruelty are soon forgotten because they consume their weak hosts as quickly as any cancer.

## Dolly

My Pop had a 7th grade education. He was a jack of all trades, but he was mainly a welder. He worked for Seller's Engineering most of his life. They built boilers on a grand scale. The boilers in the Sears Tower my Pop welded, along with a lot of others. They had to be shipped on a specially made train they welded together.

Pop was known around town for being able to weld things together that nobody else could. One time these guys came over and wanted Pop to drop a 455 cubic inch motor into a Chevy Chevette. They knew Pop wouldn't do it, so they tricked him and said, "Ed, you see this feller right here? He said there ain't a man alive that can get this motor into this car."

Pop had his own garage with every tool you can imagine.

"No kiddin?"

If Pop had a catch phrase it was that.

"That's right Ed, and he even said he'd put $1,000 saying it can't be done."

"Is that right?"

"That's what he said, Ed."

"Mmm hmm. Alright, bring it on over."

They knew in order to get Pop to do anything, all they had to say was he couldn't do it and he'd show them no matter what it took. He pulled the front end of the car out. He made a new engine box and made reinforced motor mounts because the engine ran over 500 hp. The real problem was fitting a transmission and a drive shaft for it. He sawed up a drive shaft from a Dodge truck and had it machined out so it would fit the rear end in it. He had to cut the fender wells out so the tires wouldn't scrape. It was a big job. It took him seven days to do it. He called up the man and says, "you tell that feller to come bring me my thousand clams, son."

He got paid in $100 bills.

Pop used to plow fields with his two mules for a $1 a day during the great depression. His boss, Old man Sellers was worth over $100 million. He owned a bunch of gas fields in Henrietta, Oklahoma. Every spring, Pop had to go there and repair stuff. He called it a vacation because old man Sellers paid him twice as much as normal. He drove around either in a beat-up pick-up truck or when he was wanting to go to church, he drove a 1958 Cadillac that was in perfect condition. It was a beautiful car.

Pop would load up his toolbox and tow a trailer with a car for the old man to drive when he was there. Pop took whatever scrap was at the shop and welded up stuff like this trailer. It was huge and extremely heavy. He used it for a few years until the old man bought him a brand new 'Suzu' car for his trips to Oklahoma. Pop looked at this sorry car and said he didn't need a trailer for that little car. So instead he went up to the scrap pile and picked him out some stuff. He went to the junk yard and got a Chevy rear end from Clyde for nothing because he often said: "Son, I hope I never get so low that I have to own a Ford."

Pop brought his stash of goodies home and started welding him a two-wheel dolly to put this Suzu on. He made the fenders, painted them black with some leftover paint from the body shop. Then he bought a pair of lights for $12. He painted a white strip on the fenders. It looked slick. He put spider gears in the wheels so he could turn easier.

He loaded up and headed to Henrietta. Somewhere out of Saint Louis, some man pulled up next to him on the freeway trying to get him to pull over. Pop ignored him at first but the man in the Mercedes Benz kept pointing and carrying on. Pop said: "I figured he needed a ride home since it's only about one in five Mercedes that will actually get you home without breaking down." So Pop finally pulls over.

"Son, if you need a ride home, I'll be glad to take you."

"No sir, I just wanted to look at this contraption you're using."

"You mean the dolly?"

"Is that what you call it?"

"Yes sir."

"Where'd you get it at?"

"Well son, I made it."

"Would you be willing to sell it?"

"Oh no son. I'm off to Henrietta, Oklahoma with it and I have to carry this car to my boss."

"Would you take $1,000 for it?"

Now, Pop only had $12 in the thing. He scratched his head for a minute. "Well that's a lot more than I got in it son, but I made it 'cause I need it..."

## Pocket Full of Pie

"How about $2,000? Would that get it?"

"Oh now son, I only spent my time and $12 to make it."

"I'll tell you what, if you sell it to me today, I'll give you $5,000 for it."

The man pulled out 50 $100 bills. This was in 1976.

Pop said, "well if you wanna give your money away like that, I guess I can drop this car and get a trailer for it. Pop felt like he robbed him but said the man was smiling when he let out. Pop came home and just made himself another. Everyone would come by to borrow it. He was so sick of all the people bothering him he made another just to loan out.

A couple of years later we were up at the Feed Store and there was a U-Haul Trailer rental dealership right next to it. As we were walking in, Pop walked over to where they had some new dollies on the lot. He looked it over for a few minutes.

"You reckon that feller worked for the U-Haul company son?"

"Prolly did pop."

My Pop was as ignorant as a 7th grader and blind in one eye but he was a genius in his own way.

He was my hero.

## Trouble

We lived out in the sticks in Oldham County before it became the richest county in Kentucky. My dad didn't like bussing and that's when a lot of people began to flee into what became the suburbs of Louisville. We had this lake house on Herrington Lake and like all water, it was green. There was a pool made of wood on our dock and it had a lot of moss on the wooden slats that was completely gross. If you ever slipped and got it between your nails it was absolute agony until you could get it out.

There were two movies in the 80s that made the lake scary AF - Gremlins and Friday the 13th. I can still do that Jason sound perfectly. Normally the adults were in bed by midnight because the lake was a booze paradise. It would be so hot in the summer that we would go swimming until late in the morning. At night the fish would be more active, and they would brush against you and scare the hell out of the girls.

Mom was a big Basil Rathbone fan and he made one of the Sherlock Holmes movies, The Hounds of the Baskervilles. It was an old black and white movie. I did not like black and white movies at all as a kid but not for the reasons you might think. I hated black and white movies because of the Creature from the Black Lagoon. I had nightmares about that thing swimming in the lake. It scared me so much that I didn't learn to swim until I was 13. I was not going to let one of the Gremlins or Jason or the Black Lagoon monster get me!

So when mom turned on Hounds of the Baskervilles one night, I was less than enthusiastic. In it, there are these demon dogs that are the vicious spawn of Satan that eat people and rip them to shreds. In the movie, the hounds were Rottweilers. I was a little scared of dogs then because a German Shepard bit my sister Cathy and tore a piece of flesh off her arm when she was like five or six years old. Once you get into the drama of the movie though, it's enthralling, even though it's old as can be.

When you live out in the sticks, if anyone comes out around your house, they got no business being there. One night I went down in the garage to get some tools and when I got down to the bottom of the steps, I saw the shadow of what I was convinced was Sasquatch. I ran up the steps and told mom immediately that Bigfoot was there to murder everyone.

The next day we were coming home in the Beetle mom was driving and some car pulled up next to us and was flagging us down. Turns out the car was on fire. So we got out and before long, the troopers and the fire department were there. The car was burned out completely.

We'd never had any problem with it before.

After that, mom decided to solve the problem with a couple of dogs that could handle the average Bigfoot. So we started looking for Rottweilers to make sure there were no more intruders at the Clay House. Our male was named Trouble and the female was Saiidina from the Dune book. To give you an idea how big Trouble was, we had an old truck tire in our yard that was once a swing my pop made for us. That became Trouble's chew toy. He would play with it. Toss it up in the air and run it down.

Once we had the dogs, what was really strange is that when someone would come up, they would start circling the car like Indians circling a wagon. The UPS guy never had a problem. All of our friends knew, and they would just sit by the driver's side door because they wanted to be patted on the head like the good dogs they were.

We had a gravel driveway because mom couldn't afford to pave it when she built the house. So when she had enough money to pave it, she called a few people to give estimates. Now there were a couple of times when we saw the dogs getting a little aggressive when people would get out of their car, or at least try to, and if the dogs were acting like that, mom wouldn't have anything to do with them.

If they couldn't make it past the dogs, something was wrong with them.

These contractors did not know it, but they were only going to get the bid if they could get by the dogs and had the best price. The second one to show up was this Pakistani man who came up in a red truck with white lettering on it.

As soon as this guy got to the top of the driveway and parked, the pups were circling around his truck like a bunch of Apache and they were barking like we had never heard them bark before. Trouble and Saiidina would not let him out of the truck. Trouble was lunging at the window on the driver's side. He went to the front and jumped up on the hood of his truck because we lived on the side of a hill so when you would pull up, your hood was just about level with the back yard. Trouble was just going off like I have never seen him. I heard mom call me from the window.

"Are you seeing this?"

Trouble was staring this guy down and slobbering at him like he wanted some meat. I had never seen him like this. So I went downstairs to put up Saiidina, who was also barking and circling the truck. Mom had to grab Trouble and drag him to the pen.

Finally the guy gets out and starts filling out the bid and I know he has no chance but what made him stand out to me besides the dogs were very unusual eyes. They were really green and his right one looked like his pupil had been sliced in half and he had grown another below it. I've never seen anything like it before. I'm telling you if Trouble was loose, that guy would have been torn apart.

It was about five years later when I saw that man again on television.

Mom and I were watching the news when they popped his mugshot. When the police arrived, they found him trying to drive a knife into the woman that was at his house. After they subdued him, they did a search for his house, they found 3 barrels in his basement which looked really out of place. When one of the cops opened one, they found a body.

There were three women in those barrels.

## 11 Minutes

The reason why we don't like to talk about things that make us uncomfortable is because it reminds us of old pain. There's a scene in The People vs. Larry Flynt where he is in the midst of a terrible opioid addiction and he has surgery on his back. When he wakes up with no pain, he tells Althea that their drug days are over and that he wants his mind back.

When I woke up from my brain surgery, the first thing I knew was that the pain in my eye that had tormented me so horribly for 17 years was gone. Then as the anesthesia wore off, the pain from the surgery started to radiate. My neurosurgeon ordered a post op MRI to evaluate and get a reference should the tumor come back.

I was on a lot of morphine and I had a bolus pump, so I wasn't allowed to have water. Just a few ice chips so I could only speak in whispers. The ENT surgeon had closed me up. They went in the roof of my mouth and up through my nose. He was Britney Spears' doctor so I thought, 'well she wouldn't get a bozo.'

So they take me down to the MRI. I climb on the table and the nurse hits the button to put me in the MRI. I had only gone in a couple of inches when I felt something pop. My nose was packed with 10 4x4s. Then I felt a burning sensation as if a hot poker was in my nose. The pain was just unreal. I said in my whisper: "STOP". It was a miracle the nurse heard me. She came over: "you okay sweetie?" It was the most pain I had ever been in. Tears were flowing and she said: "what's wrong?" I said: "fire."

She reversed the table and the Radiologist came over: "How are we doing over here?" I said: "Something popped, and it feels like there's fire." I was hitting that bolus pump like you can't imagine. So he walks over to the screens and picks up the phone. "Yes Dr. Stein, I'm with Thomas Clay in the MRI and he said he felt a pop in his sinuses." A brief pause. "WHAT?! Why isn't it in his chart? Dr. Morasutti ordered a post op MRI it's right there in his chart. You didn't use any metal clips, did you? He's in the fucking machine right now!"

He got up and detached the bolus pump and put the morphine bag directly into my IV and squeezed the bag. My wife called my dad to tell him what happened, and he made it from 4th and Muhammed Ali to Baptist east in his Porsche in

11 minutes. So I am laying in the pre-op ward and Dr. Stein is wanting to go in and check things out when that calvary showed up. Dad was carrying his legal pad and the anesthesiologist had rigged me a plunger of Versed with 20 mgs. I hit that plunger and pulled the covers over my head because I knew what was coming because Dad was already beet red.

What followed was one of the worst verbal lashings in all of human history. There were at least 20 patients and staff in there and my dad had reduced Dr. Stein into a 'dumb motherfucker.' Now this might seem like bad decorum but after he called him that, I looked at the nurses at the station and one cupped her hands over her mouth and two high-fived each other. My dad left all of his fucks in the Porsche. The looks on the nurses' faces was priceless.

Narcotics were the only thing that could control the pain I had. This one Radiologist had missed my tumor on MRI, twice. Once in '91 and again in '94. In 1989, I was in my room with the windows blacked out. I had these terrible headaches since I was 14 and they just kept getting more intense and more frequent. I went to 27 doctors trying to do anything to stop them. The one particular day I was in so much pain that I was on all fours and ramming my head into my wall. My mom came in and said, "what in the hell are you doing?" I told her it was a bad one. She went in her room and brought me a pill. It was as if heaven had come down and stopped the pain.

My family, except my mom, were convinced that the only thing I wanted to do was sit on my ass and take pills. This abuse went on for 11 years before I found out about the tumor. I loved rubbing it in too because they were just horrible to me. I loved tormenting the doctors who told me it was just in my head and who prescribed me antidepressants that I didn't need and injected me with cortical steroids over 200 times.

When I walked into my endocrinologist for the first time, he looked up at me and said: "oh you have some kind of pituitary adenoma, I see." I started crying because he knew at a glance what all these other assholes had missed. We talked a few minutes and he told me that he was at a PTA meeting when he saw one of the teachers with her thyroid gland about to pop out of her neck. He was Indian so he asked his wife if he should say anything to her. His wife told him not to say anything. He did say something and caught her thyroid cancer in time. He saved her life. He said: "yeah if I had seen you on the street, I would have stopped you and told you that you had a brain tumor."

I was addicted to opioids for 19 years. In the end I was doing eight 80mg Oxycontin, three 1,200 mcg of Actiq fentanyl and three 30mg oxycodone a day and sometimes double that. My doctor peeps will tell you that's enough for a herd of elephants.

You eventually get to the point where no amount of opioids can give you any relief and you're just taking the amount you are to keep from having withdrawals, which really are terrible. They're not as terrible as being a slave to a chemical. What happens to your mind is that time stops. You stop maturing because you're only worrying about not being dope sick or in pain. That's what they rob you of your life. When I was an addict, I was certain that it was better to feel nothing than the agony of existence.

But, if you manage not to overdose and die, you get to the point where you are sick and tired of being sick and tired. Some people never get to that point.

I've met a lot of very bright people who have opinions on addiction that are as useful as tits on a bull and I am including doctors in this. We have a pretty damn big problem now in this country and I have thought a great deal about this. First, there is not a simple solution to this. What we are doing is not working. It is not working, because the workarounds to the problem are what make doctors and patients alike uncomfortable. This needs incremental change and sometimes that first step is a difficult one.

The first step to fix this problem is to remove law enforcement from the equation. This is a public health matter, not a police matter. Police know one thing and that's how to lock people up. We've been doing that for decades and that's not working. Admitting the truth is the first step in recovery. If law enforcement could deal with this problem, they'd close the Chinese manufacturers making all the Fentanyl for the Mexican cartels who are buying it and flooding the US with it.

Drug enforcement is a miserable failure. Prohibition has never and will never work yet here we are again, in the midst of another prohibition and law enforcement admits that it is impotent to curtail drug use. We have to wrestle control out of the hands of CRIMINALS.

There is nothing stopping an addict from getting all the opioids they want now. If we take the police out of our doctor's offices, that would be a great improvement. We have to start changing our minds about old policies which have gotten us to the point where thousands of people are overdosing. I've seen a lot of people say: "so what? They're addicts. They don't give a shit about life." That person they are so willing to throw away is me, your friend. I have taken opioids a few times since I quit. It's a popular opinion: "once an addict always an addict." That's 12-step bullshit.

If you want things to get better in this country, then start being a better citizen. Nothing will ever get better doing the same thing over and again, yet this is what we have in the US because we've become afraid to try anything new, or worse still, admit that we were wrong.

This drug war has been a familial and societal failure and it is destroying not just families but our republic.

## Albrecht Durer

Mom was an art teacher and had a degree in Art History. Her house was really big. Packed with stuff she found at auctions. We loved auctions.

We went to this auction in Skylight once. It was in this very old mansion on the side of a cliff overlooking the Ohio river. It was a beautiful place but really run down. It had a lot of antiques in it. Stuff I'd never seen. Dolls I'd never seen. Two cars from the 40s that had been in the garage since then. Above the garage there was a Steinway baby grand made of Brazilian rosewood and ivory keys. It was bought for a daughter who died very young. It was in absolute mint condition. It was like walking into a time capsule.

There were Tiffany lamps. Exotic guns. This stuff was good enough to be at Sotheby's. There was a bronze Buddha fountain. They had really old furniture from China. There was a Persian rug that was 12X14. I wish I had a picture of it so you could appreciate how beautiful it was. There were a couple of Indian/Persian rug dealers there. When you deal in antiques, you never want anyone to know how much money you have so the really rich dealers drove old pick-up trucks because they didn't want anyone to run up the bid on them. The Indian/Persian guys were in a new Mercedes and a Rolls Royce.

I knew there was going to be fireworks.

The highest priced rug I'd seen before went for $3,000. They started the bidding at $1,000 and usually they go up in $500 increments. The Indian guy started. The Persian said: "$5,000". I hadn't seen anything like that. The Indian goes: "$10,000." The auctioneer was in heaven. The Persian went: "$20,000." They slowed down at $40,000. Back and forth they went. The Persian won it at $52,500.

They started in the house, so we went outside to the box lots. Mom had on cheap jeans and a blouse with a $500 crystal broach. You'd think she was homeless, but she also had $10,000 cash on her. So mom is rummaging through the box lots. I'm completely disinterested when I see her stop, shuffle something to the bottom and put a napkin over the box lot. She stands up and she's looking both ways as if she'd just found a brick of cocaine and five bundles of cash in it.

She comes over to me like a cat with a canary in her mouth.

"There's an Albrecht Durer Bunny engraving in there."

"Who is Albert Durer?"

"He's the greatest engraver there ever was you dumb son of a bitch!"

"You just called yourself a bitch."

So about two hours later it's time for the box lots. In the meantime, this interior designer had spotted it. The question was, was this a print Durer actually did or was it a reprint? Well she didn't have a degree in Art History, and mom did.

It was the real deal.

You also need to understand my mom was as cheap as can be but she wanted this, badly. The bidding started at $5. Mom raised her hand the first bid. The interior designer bid $100. This is considered bad manners which elicited a 'fucking bitch' from mom. "I'll show her!"

"$500."

"$1,000." If mom had had a knife, she would have been cut.

"$2,000." I'm like, 'gulp.' Mom had clearly lost her mind.

"$2,500." Mom goes: "I thought that'd slow you down bitch. She doesn't know if it's real."

When the hammer dropped, mom got it for $2,850. It was from the 1400s. She thought it was serendipitous because it was her birthday.

She wanted me to remember her every year on her birthday, which is today.

I sure do miss her a bunch.

# Gary

Her pupils were fixed and dilated when I found her.

Gary had been living with me for around six months, maybe longer. I didn't keep track. Jennifer worked with him at Tumbleweed. She was a beautiful woman, and the new upscale location of Louisville's favorite Mexican restaurant suited her. She had gotten out of rehab and wanted to get her kid back. She was only thirty-three years old. Her mom lived in Tennessee. That was all I knew about her.

The night before, Gary had taken her out to Wick's pizza. It took me years to get over what happened.

"What could I have done differently?"

"What if I had done this?"

"What if I had done that?"

She had already been staying in Gary's room downstairs for over two weeks, so that night I didn't pay much attention to the time when I heard them come in. All of a sudden Jen was walking into my bedroom and taking her clothes off. She was really drunk.

I found Gary and told him that he should take his girlfriend to bed and let her sleep it off. If I had known what I know now, I would have shot him in the head. Gary and I had two things in common, we didn't drink and we both loved playing pool. I had the best setup money could buy and he was a good player but a truly vile man as it turned out.

At the time, I was having trouble sleeping anyway, and an intoxicated naked woman in my bed wasn't helping. I had already taken my sleeping meds and Gary weighed about 115 pounds soaking wet, so the question was how we were going to get her down to Gary's bed. She wasn't in any frame of mind to help, and I felt pretty sure she and Gary had been smoking weed. They both loved it, and I hated it, and I always thought that was about all they saw in each other. Anyway, we waited around for about twenty minutes and I finally scooped her up and carried her downstairs and put her in bed.

I've had a somewhat sheltered life and the way I was raised, touching an intoxicated woman was an extreme violation of the gentleman's code. A day or two earlier, Jen had mentioned that she had a court date about her daughter the next morning. I normally slept until noon, but that morning, I woke up at 7:00 to piss. As I was commencing, I remembered that Jen had a court date and I realized I could wake her up and be sure she got there.

So I went downstairs to wake her up and she was sprawled out naked and I saw white stuff coming out of her mouth. Gary was ~~laying~~ lying next to her when the adrenaline hit.

"CALL 911!" I screamed.

Her left pupil was dilated all the way. In my head I knew that was brain damage, but I didn't think, I just reacted. I checked for a pulse. I couldn't feel any. She wasn't cold. I tried 3 quick breaths, but nothing went through. I did a finger sweep and got the vomit out of her mouth. I finally got some breaths in her.

I started chest compressions but basically I was just pushing her into the mattress. By then, Gary was on the phone, and I screamed out the address because Gary didn't know. I don't know how long it took for them to get there but everything was in slow motion. My back began cramping badly so I told Gary to take over. I stood erect and it got better quickly. Gary was just bouncing her on the mattress. I put her on the floor and straddled her like they teach you in CPR class. 1-2-3 chest compressions, one breath.

I told Gary to wait outside for the ambulance. Those few minutes before they arrived still haunt me. I stared into her lifeless eyes. "Don't go Jen. Please don't go. Please. Don't go Jen." The lactic acid was building to the point I couldn't do anymore. I saw the door open. "GET THE PADDLES!" The other one came over. "Take over for me." I collapsed on my back. His colleague came running in with the defibrillator.

They hit her three times with it. Nothing. They were shaking their heads like they were calling it. "One more time. Please." I begged.

They tried again, and something happened. The one on top of her called for the big needle. He put the adrenaline in her heart. I heard the monitor beep a few times. They put her on the stretcher and ran her out of there.

They "called her" eight hours later.

What Gary didn't tell me was that she had drunk twenty-six shots of Crown Royal. That's more than a liter of alcohol in a 128-pound woman. At autopsy, her blood alcohol level was .46. The coroner called me a couple of days later. He was a friend of my dad's. He told me she had consumed some pills too. He asked to speak to Gary and I listened in as he told the coroner what happened the night before. I won't say what I heard but when they were done, I came out of my room holding my pistol and told Gary to get the fuck out of my house. It was a good thing I never saw him again.

I didn't find out until years later that Gary was the last person to see my ex-wife Lisa alive. Her mother found her unconscious on Christmas Eve with a broken nose. She was apparently extremely drunk. They got Lisa to the hospital, but her kidneys had shut down. She died on the twenty seventh.

Gary told Lisa's parents that I was the reason Jen died.

The day I learned Lisa had died was over two years after she passed. She was only 40. I was overwhelmed with grief. I wanted to do something. I cried for her mother because they had a peculiar closeness that was positively supernatural. Lisa closed the car door on her finger once and it wasn't five seconds later her mom called and said, "what happened? Is she okay?"

I called her parents in tears. I wouldn't be that prick that didn't call.

"Lewis, it's Thomas. I just found out. I am so sorry. She was such a beautiful woman." Whatever hostility he felt those two years melted away. We shared that grief and I felt it pour out of him as he told me what happened. Her mom knew something wasn't right with Gary's story. I told him what really happened with Jennifer. Lewis told me he thought a lot more of me because I called and things made more sense now.

Sometimes, you just need to get things off your chest so you can move on with your life.

## Judy

I could ask him what her name was. I know he knows it, my dad, because It was his first really big case. Memory is so strange as you get older. You can never tell a young person that. Some things seem a thousand years ago: a happy memory, vacations, the first time you make love, the first time you kiss a girl.

I remember that one.

Her name was Judy Carrico. She lived four houses down from our house. I wanted her to be my girlfriend. I remember walking to school with her and carrying her books. She had two red barrettes in her honey-colored hair, and she was the cutest girl in the world. It was sometime just after Mom's birthday in June, 1975.

Old man Smitty was the street grouch, who was always drinking Falls City beer and screaming at us kids to get off his lawn. That day all the kids were playing hide-and-seek, and Judy and I were hiding under the two big hedges in Smitty's front yard. I had five pieces of Bazooka Joe bubble gum and while we sat behind the bush, I gave her one and then it happened. She kissed me. The moon and stars parted for a few moments and Angels might as well have been singing Ode to Joy.

I remember it was murderously hot that summer. We had an apple tree in the back yard with a huge bees nest in it and that I went to great lengths to avoid it.

I remember wanting to see Judy the next day, and I remember running out back to see what Dad and Harley were doing. Harley was a bald-headed tattooed biker who was scary to look at, but he played kickball with me so I liked him.

I saw Dad and Harley cleaning a strange green car. It was the day I heard a word I had never heard before.

Murder.

Dad is a lawyer and if you know the breed, they are quite, shall we say…" clinical" about certain things. Dad is brilliant; he has a genius IQ and a memory like Rain Man. Dad had a client who had murdered someone. I didn't know what "murder" meant. He said, "Well, son, he was going across the

Second Street bridge and took a 12-gauge shotgun and blew her head off." Dad was never one to pussyfoot around.

I could smell Dad's cologne before I saw what he and Harley were doing. I thought they were just washing the car but what they were doing was washing out the car. I used to have nightmares about it. The smell of liquefying flesh in the June sun is something you never forget. It was a new car, worth a lot of money, and it was my dad's payment for representing the murderer. The damn thing should have been burned.

"Give us a hand, boy."

I remember watching Pulp Fiction the first time and seeing the scene where Vincent Vega shoots Marvin in the back of the car. The long-gone nightmares of my youth had come back. The car we had cleaned out was exactly like that one–only worse because it was real.

Blood and horror have never been an abstract idea for me. I learned it scraping some woman's brains out of the back of a car. I am acutely and intimately familiar with it. To this day, the smell of English Leather makes me nauseous. I hate it.

I watched while the two attorneys for the mass murderers in California began to suggest that Sandy Hook was a false flag operation and I thought to myself, 'I bet they wouldn't say that shit if they had to look at the bodies with congealed blood forming stalactites and stalagmites made out of blood and brain matter.' That kind of paranoia plays well, at least to their audience.

Cowardice, like stupidity, has seeped into the national swamp where cold-blooded lying malefactors with slime coursing through their veins feast on the blood of the innocents. Children have been slaughtered as these cowardly whores–I refuse to call them men because they aren't–sent thoughts and prayers and took blood money from the National Rifle Association.

None of those sorry sons of bitches had the balls to go to Newtown and meet the families of the murdered children. The NRA spends tens of millions of dollars each election and they get everything they want and then some. Every single Republican in Congress and even a few Democrats, take the money and send prayers.

They never have to bury any of their own.

When their colleague Gabby Gifford was shot in the head, they sent thoughts and prayers. When Charleston happened, more thoughts and prayers. When Colorado Springs happened, more thoughts and prayers. Roseburg, thoughts and prayers. Chattanooga, thoughts and prayers. Isla Vista, thoughts and prayers. Washington DC, thoughts and prayers. Do we send thoughts and prayers when a house is on fire? Do we send thoughts and prayers when someone is having a heart attack?

For astute legal observers, there was a Supreme Court case in 2007 called District of Columbia vs. Heller. Conservatives always cite 'judicial activism' when they lose a case they think they should win. However, Heller was decided 5-4 with Scalia writing the majority decision. The Court voted to extend the right to bear arms, clearly limited by the Constitution to a standing militia, to any citizen. Those "judicially inactive" conservatives abrogated two hundred years of Constitutional Law, written by previous Justices. I imagine Wayne LaPierre strangling hookers in a DC hotel from the glee of buying his minions on a Supreme Court that does his bidding.

It is rare for any judge to critique a Supreme Court decision because they are often hoping to be appointed to the Court themselves, but not Richard Posner, the prominent Reagan-appointed federal appellate judge:

At a moment in modern America when more than 30,000 lives are lost to gun violence each year and mass shootings are a common occurrence, the majority opinion relied heavily on a guesstimate (and a rotten one at that) of what the Second Amendment meant more than 200 years ago, with no common-sense balancing test taking into account the real-world consequences for today."

We're the only nation in the world that suffers this amount of "Megadeath," unrelated to nuclear holocaust. More people have been killed with guns than have died in every war of the 20th century. I hear too many straw-man arguments like, "Cars kill more people than guns; are we going to outlaw cars?" This year, cars have, just barely, killed more people than guns. But Explorers are not specifically designed to kill the neighbor's boy walking through my yard at midnight, and even souped up T'Birds don't kill 30,000 people a year; guns do. How did we get this far?

As I read that Heller decision, I remembered what Malcom X said nearly 60 years ago: "When a house is built upon a weak foundation composed of lies, it will eventually crumble and fall." When Supreme Court Justices are lying to do the bidding of the NRA, we don't have long as a nation before the purging flames of revolution begin to baptize traitors like Wayne LaPierre and the rows of conservative whores on the Supreme Court and in congress.

The only difference between the US and everyone else is the sheer amount of cheap unregulated guns and ammunition. The NRA has appealed to the paranoia and patriotism of their constituents to convince them that bearing arms is what keeps our government from tyranny and our citizens safe, and they beat that drum incessantly.

Intransigence has a cost and a deadly one at that. The problem of course is that the entire NRA narrative is but an abstract idea that appeals to fear and it works great. Wayne has done well for his gun manufacturer sponsors who profit so egregiously whenever these mass murders happen and panic-stricken people flock to gun stores to buy more weapons.

As Frank Herbert put it, 'fear is the mind killer'; it's an addictive poison that the NRA and Fox News supply in doses just strong enough to get people to forget what this country is all about. In case these flag-waving, gun-toting hatriots aren't aware of it, Fox News, one of the purveyors of all that fear and rage, is owned by an Australian and a Saudi Prince. Fox's daily menu is a narcotic that permits people to shrug and look away when twenty toddlers are mowed down with an Army gun and to consider Sandy Hook just a false flag operation.

The one incontrovertible truth about those Alex Jones types is that they've never seen the autopsy photos. They're not going to clean up any blood, but they will send those cold-blooded, unethical NRA reprobates back to congress with thoughts and prayers to the families of the victims so long as their right to murder twenty people with $4 worth of ammunition is not impeded in any way.

If history has taught us anything through the ages, it's this: Introduce a little fear and a country will tear itself apart, which is something Joe McCarthy knew all too well. They only have to feed our fears and we will overreact, predictably and with deadly precision. We will find our scapegoats and load our weapons, and one of those men will ride those fears all the way to the White House if we sit idly by and do nothing.

Late at night, I think about the jubilation I felt when Judy kissed me and how rudely the cruelty of life visited me as a boy when I was cleaning up the remnants of a body from a woman I never knew. She had such a profound impact on my life because I could never enjoy seeing it through a prism where blood and brains didn't matter. Her death was a cruel awakening to the depravity of man, and I learned right then and there that no problem is ever solved with a gun. That's what she taught me, and I shed a few tears for her humanity because I'll never know her name.

## Lance

If I ever had a brother, his name was Lance. We grew up in the same city. Worked together as busboys. Both kids of professional parents who had money.

Lance and I were peanut butter and jelly.

He had this house once and it was just absolutely falling apart. I knew how to do carpentry and rebuild houses. So we needed to tear the entire back half of this house off and redo the bathroom and the kitchen. When we got done we were sitting in where the basement is looking up in the sky and smoking a cigarette where a roof should have been.

Lance didn't have grandparents, but he knew mine and they loved him like their own. He would drive all the way up to Danville and visit. He'd come in at 3 am and just walk on in. At some point he started banging my little sister and things got weird between us. We couldn't talk about pussy anymore. He borrowed my Pop's truck once and we were driving home to his mom's place and I had to piss like you wouldn't believe. So he is driving like 30 MPH and veering off into the emergency lane to run over the potholes to cause me more pain. Someone called the cops on us and said we were drunk driving.

The cops pull us over and this happens to be in a city which my dad had sued twice and won over $10 million from. They didn't have the money to buy squad cars because my dad took all their money. I got pulled over all the time and they would see my name and start fucking with me because of my dad. So Lance pulls over and I am about to piss myself. The cops tell me to get out. I could run to his apartment and piss from where I was, but the cops wouldn't let me. I finally tell them I have to piss and he was driving that way to try and make me piss and Lance is just rolling the entire time.

So something happened between Lance and my sister and I didn't know at the time what it was. Turns out he got her pregnant and she had an abortion. Lance wasn't really religious, but his parents were super Catholic. All I knew was that him and Anne were broke up. Now I have to mention at this point that Lance was a very handsome dude and he had a huge dick. So we get done working on his house and his dad is all proud that he made a bunch of money on it and what not. we were still bussing tables and there was this little short thing with a magnificent ass that Lance was really interested in. So he started dating Amy. She was from Memphis.

Now Amy just loved Lance. She would go shopping with his sister and baby sit for free. She'd go shopping with his mom and carry groceries in and she was just loved by everyone. The problem was that me and Lance spent more time together than she got to because we didn't need her doing construction together. Amy didn't like me much because I was the honcho at the restaurant and when something wasn't working, I made sure it worked.

So this brain tumor I had prevented me from having any sex hormones although I didn't know it at the time so I didn't chase women like most men did and I talk 'funny' according to any hick I run into and well, Amy concluded that I was gay and she told Lance's mother this. We normally stayed at his mom's place on work nights because I lived way out in the country. So we get up one day and his mom made breakfast and she says, "I think there's too much togetherness."

I groaned when she said it because I knew who put that in her ear. If I could go back in time in my life, I would go back to that moment and try to undo it more than anything in my life.

So Amy got what she wanted, a lot more time with Lance.

Amy liked to drink and party and have fun. I never drank and all Lance and I did together was work. This kinda threw a wrench into all that we were doing because Amy needed dick time. There was another girl working there named Bunny. Bunny was about one of the most beautiful women there was, and one night they were all at a party and Lance's dick kinda fell into Bunny. So one thing led to another and they broke up and Lance started going with Bunny.

Well Bunny liked to party even harder than Amy, and one night Lance totaled his Z24 on his way home. Lance's mom had this bar with slot machines in it and one day we were over helping her count her money and she had $264,000 in cash under the bed. She couldn't very well do anything with all this cash, so she just handed Lance the cash to fix his car.

Lance had a temper problem anyway and when he would get drunk, it was so much worse. But Lance was an affable guy and Bunny and Lance were just the cutest. So one day Joe invited them out to Churchill Downs to go have some cocktails and such and one day Lance won like $8,000 on a race. Joe introduced Lance to the Long Island Ice Teas which graduated him from beer to hard liquor.

I think it was about the 4th time Lance had totaled a car when I sat him down and we had a talk. You see we had this guy named John who bussed with us. One night he was out hot dogging around drinking beer with his best friend in the world in his Datsun 240 ZX and he lost control and killed his best friend. This was a huge media case in Louisville and the prosecutor in his case was a real shithead. So John has a curfew and he is working with us and one night he worked just a few minutes too late and he broke his curfew by 5 minutes. So this prick prosecutor tries to impose his sentence. John was also a star athlete with a football scholarship. So shit got really ugly for John and what was so fucked up about it was that the few times John ever talked about it, he broke down and cried: "I killed my best friend man. I killed my best friend."

So there I am talking to Lance about all this drunk driving he's getting away with and I remind him about John. For a few minutes there, we were back to being brothers and I told him I didn't care where he was, I didn't care what time it was, I wanted him to call me if he was drunk and I would come get him and he knew I meant it because we loved one another. He swore he would.

We drifted apart. He was at mom's funeral. He wasn't good at grief, but he was there. I soon married my old girlfriend and was making a life with her. I went up to see Granny and Pop and Lance was there once. I was in the shower and he would turn off the hot water and start singing this stupid song, 'HOT SHOWER! DON'T YOU WISH YOU COULD HAVE A HOT SHOWER!' He sang it like this Lebanese waiter we worked with. We locked him in the basement once and waited on all of his tables so that nobody even knew he was there. We gave him all the tips too. He would see a horse race and be shouting at the top of his lungs, "Whip him boy! Whip him goddamnit!" We fucked with each other like that. When I'd be working on something, I could reach behind me and he'd hand me the exact tool I needed. Esprit De' Corps doesn't really cut how close we were. He was my brother. I would have died or killed for him. My nephew is named for him.

Where I lived in Oldham County, I was in the flight path of the Life Flight helicopter that would fly from the University of Louisville Trauma Center to the Tri-county hospital in Lagrange. The stretch of highway in front of my mom's house had taken 16 lives. Three of whom I watched take their last breaths. The smell of alcohol was overwhelming in all of them. Four teenagers at the local high school died and after that, they finally put in guard rails.

I was painting our laundry room gray that day. I quit at about 2 am. I happened to be watching "A River Runs Through It" when I drifted off to sleep.

I heard it coming in.

When I would hear that chopper coming and pass, I would say a prayer, 'God, if you're up there, help that person in their time of need.' I started saying it as I heard it coming only this time, something was different. It came in low. It was so low that it shook the pictures off my wall. I had a big Galileo thermometer on top of my TV, and it fell and I was just shocked it didn't break. It passed over my house and landed about a mile down the road. Whoever it was, didn't get to the hospital so I knew this was a bad one. They flew right over my house on the way back.

The few people who had my phone number knew never to call me in the morning or I would be really pissed. I opened my right eye when I heard the call. The clock said 7:13. I jumped to get call. Time stood still as I looked at the caller ID. It was Page, Lance's sister. I knew instantly it was Lance.

I answered, "Is he alive?'

"Barely. We're at University."

I don't even remember putting my shoes on but I remember doing 155 mph in my Porsche all the way down I-71. I was crying the whole way. When I got to the trauma ward, the elevator opened, and I saw his mom first. Paige was standing by the door.

"The doctors are in there now. He's not in any pain. His spine was severed at C2. He doesn't want to see you.'

There were at least twelve very attractive women there all just sobbing. Paige knew more than anyone, he needed me.

He had his eyes closed when I walked in. He had 4 screws in his head holding 60 pounds of traction. They were trying to save his ability to breathe on his own. I grabbed his hand, sobbing uncontrollably. He opened his eyes. He looked to his left. The tears were the worst fucking thing I ever saw. He was all hopped up on morphine so he had no voice. I had never hurt like this. My soul was crushed. So was his. I would have done ANYTHING to take that awful reality from his eyes.

He looked up at me and started mouthing, 'If you love me, kill me.'

It was the worst fucking moment of my life because he knew I loved him.

"I can't. I can't. Please don't ever ask me that."

Because he knew I was the only one that would, and it still crushes my soul that I could not do that. I wanted to take his place because I would have been better suited for it. I would have done anything to make it go away and the others out in the waiting room would have done it, they loved him that much too.

So yeah, I'd tell the people I love anything at all or use any trick to keep them or me from Lance's fate and I'd do the same damn thing for you if it would break your addiction. I don't want to ever get the call where something bad happens to someone and I have to call their mother and tell her bad news.

## Lyssa

My Granny was a master seamstress. When she was growing up in Crab Orchard during the great depression, she had to wear potato sacks to go to school. She caught Scarlett fever when she was six. She could barely hear with hearing aids. She would cry as she told me about wearing potato sacks and how the kids made fun of her. I have always hated bullies.

She made shoes at a factory for a lot of years. The plant shut down and she got one of the industrial sewing machines that sewed leather together. Everything she wore was tailor made to fit. I still have a welding cap she made for my Pop. She made Pop's billfolds. He lost his billfold once. It slipped out of his bib overalls when he was changing a power steering hose in a broke down friend's car up by the Holiday Inn in Danville.

By the time he realized it, it was dark so he went looking for it. We went back up to the Holiday Inn. It wasn't there. He was really upset about it. The next day someone came knocking on the door with his billfold. A random woman found it and just brought it back to him. He pulled out a $20 bill and handed it to her.

"Oh no Mr. Waits I couldn't. You cut my Mawmaw's grass for free."

"Just you take it."

If you searched Pop's wallet you would have trouble finding the 20 $100 bills he kept in it in the secret compartment. He carried a lot of cash in case he needed to buy something on sale.

Mom had one of the first mediport models that came onto the market to get her chemo in. It was right in the center of her chest. Mom told me she was sick one night, so I took her temperature and it was 99 degrees. Not unusual so I asked if she was having a White Castle attack? She didn't want to eat. The next morning I go to check on her and I can tell something is wrong. I took her temp and it was 102.1 and she couldn't breathe.

She hated going to the hospital, but she knew something was up. So I load her up and go to the ER.

That was the day I met Bonnie and Lyssa.

Her name was Clarissa but she went by Lyssa. She was next to us in the ER. They brought Lyssa in on a stretcher and she was crying in agony. She was just seven years old. Bonnie was in tears.

The doctor asked Bonnie: "what happened?"

"She was running around the couch with her brother and she fell and started screaming."

"Did she run into something?"

"No she was just playing and this happened."

"Well I've never seen a kid snap their femur like that before."

His tone was accusatory. He ordered her some morphine. Her leg was just beyond contorted. It was gruesome.

The doctor paged an orthopedic surgeon and checked on mom. He ordered a chest X-ray. It took about ten minutes to get the machine set up. Mom had a huge infection around her mediport. They called in Dr. Aaron who put it in. While we waited, the orthopedic surgeon came in. I just remember him saying, "wow."

Dr. Aaron came in just after and he saw Mom's X-ray and said, "why isn't she in the OR?" He was known to be a prick of the highest order, but you wanted him to be your doctor because he did not put up with mediocrity.

When Dr. Aaron came out of the OR, he was covered in blood from mom. When he opened her up, blood and pus sprayed all over him. She was really sick. He told me if we had waited any longer, she'd be dead. To close the wound, he had to pack it. He asked me if I could get him a steak to go from Del Frisco's, extra rare.

"How can you eat?"

"Surgery makes me hungry."

There were 26 4x4 bandages in the wound. It was in the center of mom's chest and it was just like a hole 6 inches wide and 6 inches deep. She was in intensive care for a week.

Dr. Aaron came in and goes, "do you think you can pack this wound every day?"

"I reckon."

"Well you can go home but don't leave one in there or she'll get sick again."

Apparently, it was against hospital policy to release a patient from intensive care. There was some kind of kerfuffle at the nurse's station when the entire floor heard,

"I don't give a good goddamn what the hospital policy is. She's my patient and she's going home." "

He was a great doctor.

Pulling hospital duty is arduous work. I used to cut tobacco when it was 95+ degrees and I would rather do that than pull hospital duty, which is why I always did it. I wanted to keep the "practicing" of medicine to a minimum.

The routine was mom would do 5 days of carboplatinol in the hospital once a month. I would read until my eyes went cross and then go play with the kids across the hall. I first did it out of boredom, but I quickly learned how badly these kids needed stimuli of any kind.

I haven't been in combat so that is the one caveat I give when I say the worst place in the world is any cancer ward for children. Few parents can handle it. Some can't at all. You find out who people are in a crisis. You also learn to spot the good nurses. They run everything. I don't know how they do it. I knew which ones who had done it the most because they are the most distant and cold.

They have to be.

I hate the smell of the cancer ward. It smells like faint piss and fungicide chemicals. Mom would smell it and start barfing. Same with the awful food they served. Before mom could get into her room, I would have to go spray an entire can of glade so mom could go in there without barfing. You get into a routine that even the nurses know when you do chemo for as long as mom did.

The next chemo session as I walked in to spray the lavender scented Glade, I spotted Bonnie in the kids ward. She had extremely bright red hair. As I rounded the nurse's station it hit me. I saw Lyssa in the bed with her leg in some contraption suspended above the bed. I hoped for those few seconds that they were just out of beds, then it dawned on me. I went and got mom and carried the suitcase to our room.

I was tearing up when my eyes met Bonnie's. The chemo bags have this ultraviolet light cover on them. I glanced at her IV and saw that awful bag. Bonnie saw my tears and just hugged me.

"Hi, I'm Thomas."

"I remember you from the night we came in."

"What kind is it?" I knew before I asked.

"Osteosarcoma."

I would have preferred being stabbed.

I don't know what the mortality rate for osteosarcoma in 1989 was but I knew death was certain and a painful one at that. This wasn't my first rodeo with sick kids. My little sister had AML leukemia when she was 16. That's the worst kind. She was on the kids ward for almost 2 years doing 6 days of chemo stints. She would fall asleep because her blood counts were often zero. She was doing the strongest chemo there was at that time.

Bonnie was wearing a Waffle House uniform. I could tell she came from work to sit with Lyssa. I told her to go home. I'd look after her. Hospital duty is stressfully tedious. The things that matter to the patients are the little things. Changing the channel. Sometimes calling the nurse takes more strength than they have. A cup of ice cream, getting a coke and wanting a sprite. An ice cap or anything is amplified that much more when you can't do something for yourself and you don't want to impose on a busy nurse.

Lyssa was one of those little girls who put a twinkle in your eye. One of the tumors she had was in her femur. The orthopedic surgeon opened her leg and saw what he was dealing with. He called in another oncological surgeon and there just wasn't much they could do. For most cancer patients, having a surgical option gave you a much better result, usually. For Lyssa, she only had radiation and chemo as an option.

Bonnie had no idea what she was in for. She had a son too, and rent. She'd find out soon enough. Radiation is the worst, especially for kids. It makes you so sick. You vomit out stuff that looks exactly like antifreeze. You think you can eat something, and you get it down and ten minutes later you barf it back up. You barf so much that sometimes you get ulcers on your esophagus and the acid in your stomach causes you incredible pain.

Lyssa was bed bound. The radiation kept her femur from healing. She was always in pain, but she would have good days. She liked playing chutes and ladders and watching the Muppets. Bonnie worked. Came to the hospital. Went home. Cooked dinner. Went to bed and repeated. She would have been there every moment if she could. Bonnie aged ten years in those months. When you have cancer or are caring for someone with it, every single day is a crisis because time is so precious.

About the 5th month, Lyssa was really tired from the chemo and radiation. She was more lethargic. I'd seen this before.

It was a few days after Lyssa's 8th birthday. She had a Strawberry Shortcake doll cake. Pop and Granny came down to check on mom. Keeping Pop away from cake was impossible. He always had peanut brittle, two cakes, cookies and hard candy at his house but he also used to bring us a "goodie sack" full of candy. When he'd come to the hospital he'd walk into the kids' ward and say, "Does anybody in heah like Reese's cups?" Then he'd empty the sack for the kids.

Lyssa had strawberry blonde hair, but it had all fallen out. Granny bought some wigs for her. Lyssa had eight candles to blow out. It took her a few tries to get them all out.

"This sure is awful good cake. Who's got the birthday money?" Pop called out.

Bonnie had no idea what that meant but me and mom did.

Pop pulled out his billfold and unzipped the secret compartment. He counted out.

"One. Two. Three. Five. Oops. I miscounted. Let me start over." He left the four bills and started again. He finally got to eight, all 20 $100 bills were on the table. He handed them to Bonnie.

"Now when you get out, your mama will have them waiting on you so you can get some candy," he told Lyssa with a smile. Only Pop knew she wasn't going to get out. Bonnie was in tears. Granny slipped her a check for $5,000 more.

Three weeks later I walked in and Lyssa asked me to play chutes and ladders. She was so weak. I got out the board and she matter-of-factly said: "I'm not going to make it Thomas." I froze for a moment and couldn't look her in the eyes. My eyes were leaking. She patted me on the hand.

"Don't be sad. I get to go to heaven."

"I know angel, I know."

I was fast asleep the next night when I heard this guttural and primal wailing coming from across the hall. It was Bonnie. It still haunts my nightmares from time to time, that sound. I wish I had a recording of it for whenever someone says we can't afford universal healthcare but they're "pro-life" because none of them know what the hell they are talking about.

## Mr. Randall

Beat cops must be disarmed. By acquitting all these murderous bastards, other cops have learned they can kill an unarmed black person, plant evidence on them on video and still get away with it.

As a society, we are showing generations of black kids that they are more valuable to us as prisoners and that their lives are worthless. We have allowed this militarization of our police departments to the point where they are armed with everything they want, except intellect.

If I am ever called to jury duty again, I will not vote to convict any person of color unless it's murder, child abuse or rape. This is our fault, white people. We sat by and did nothing while people of color were subjected to injustice after injustice. I remember being appalled by all the black people who celebrated OJ's verdict because I was insulated inside the cocoon of white privilege.

Let me tell you about a seminal moment in my life.

My dad had a client who had embezzled $1.2 million from a construction company he worked for so he could go gambling. He was also one of those holier-than-thou Christians. His parents could afford my dad.

The owner of the company hanged himself in his bathroom so his family would have his life insurance money. When his wife found his body dangling, she tried to get him down and she had a massive heart attack which nearly killed her. She's permanently disabled.

Everyone lost their job. The company had to file bankruptcy and everything including their home was sold.

So we go into circuit court for final sentencing and the judge has all the prisoners in chains before him and he is sentencing this black man. He had been convicted for the 3rd time for crack cocaine. He had been caught with 2 grams for this offense and this was his 3rd strike. I will never forget what he said.

"Mr. Randall, you're a menace to society and since this is your 3rd strike, I sentence you to 25 to life."

How much are two grams of cocaine worth to American citizens? Well if it's prison money, it's worth about $40,000 a year for 25 years. That's a million dollars.

Then the judge called up my dad. My dad had worked out a plea where <u>his</u> client would get seven years of probation and restitution. Restitution was 10% of his gross income until he had repaid the entirety of the $1.2 million. He worked at Kentucky Fried Chicken.

That's when the injustice really began to gnaw at my conscience because my dad's client should have died in prison, but he was white, and his parents could afford a good lawyer. His actions destroyed people's lives. That black man used some cocaine.

Who did more harm?

Our justice system is absolutely corrupt. Justice rarely comes out of it and every day in this country, innocent black men and women are killed because none of us want to confront the fact that we are complicit in their murders.

How do we fix this? Every single police department in the country must have a civilian review board with the ability to fire cops. That might get them interested in de-escalating these situations. It is departmental policy across the country to not hire intelligent cops who score high on entrance exams because they tend not to remain cops.

That policy attracts the worst of us, not the best.

Let's start taking civil judgments from the police retirement fund. I have a feeling that'll magically inspire these bastards to stop killing unarmed black people. Who knows? Maybe they'll even actually start policing the bad apples.

I am beyond sick of this shit and I will never again enjoy the view from my white privilege. It was Machiavelli who said: "a true patriot hates injustice in his own land more than anything." I will never remain silent or cooperate with this evil.

## War

"I, we."

In my experience, every single person who has exalted patriotism to make a point doesn't have a point worth remembering. I've often heard: "my brother died for your right to be free!" Some of us would prefer to die for the greater good than to die some other way. Dying for your country is one of the greatest recruiting tools the armed services have to lure young men into serving.

I met Mike when I was 15 working at a restaurant whose owners my dad represented. He was quiet. The first year he would just say: "2 coffees A4." He loved gin. He had a very deep bass voice that was difficult to hear sometimes in a busy restaurant. Everyone got a shift drink and his was always a 'Bombay rocks.'

Everyone told me Mike was quiet because he was in Vietnam. In 30 years, I never once heard him raise his voice in anger. His dad was never around, and his mom had six children. She was overwhelmed and couldn't feed all of them, so she surrendered Mike and his brother to the state. The state put them in an orphanage where they were beaten every day. The kids had to bail hay on the farm. There was a lot of other horrible things, too. He was drafted into the Marines in 1967. He said: "Hell I would have volunteered if it would have gotten me the hell out of that place!" Straight from the orphanage to a bus headed to Paradise Island. In his chronic thirst for understatement he said: "It was a bit of an adjustment."

On the night of January 30, 1968, he was at a Forward Marine outpost south of Danang. An outpost consists of a central bunker with four bunkers forming a perimeter. Mike told me his side was facing a hill they had mined with trip flares and claymore mines. Each outpost had an M60 machine gun, a mortar, and boxes of ammo they used to make furniture from. Mike was the supply sergeant, so he said he'd get 3-4 bottles of pain med bottles with 1000 pills in each and he always paid extra for some 'Thai stick' pot. They had a lot of feral pigs that would set off the trip flares which was great because they always ate really well. Each post had five men in them and it wasn't in 'the shit' as he said, 'until the shit finds you.'

## Pocket Full of Pie

It took him 25 years to tell me this story.

The hill they were facing was impossible terrain to navigate. It was jungle and they had planted over 1,000 mines on that hill. There was 50 yards of space between the bottom of the hill and the 'wire' where the outpost was. They had 300 claymore mines wired to plungers in the bunkers. I asked him how much ammo he had in his bunker.

"The other guys had about 25 crates but I dug out mine so I had 50 crates because digging wasn't hard when you're all hopped up on Benzedrine. You can hardly hear anything at night 'cause the insects are so thick. They weren't so loud this night." The way they laid out the hill was to put the trip flares higher up and the mines lower down. The first flare went off at 12 am. Then another, and another. Then they all went off." The shit had arrived, en masse.

It was the Tet Offensive.

An entire division came over that hill and was coming right at Mike. "They slowed down a tad when they hit the mines." The entire hill looked like it was moving. "People talk about Marines being really dumb but one thing we do well is lay down artillery. When those 155s (howitzers) started landing, we sobered up fast, but those little bastards kept coming. When they got to the claymores, I knew we were in trouble." They went through a mine field with over 1,000 mines.

My dad was a tank commander. I went on maneuvers with him once and he told me to stand about ten yards from this M1A1 Abrams tank. The concussion knocked me back about five feet on my ass and it felt like I was slammed in the gut with a baseball bat held by Frank Thomas. That was only a 125mm howitzer. Dad and his buddies thought it was knee-slapping funny.

The M60 is a belt-fed machine gun that spits out 500-600 rounds per minute. The command bunker had a .50 cal machine gun that was also firing. Mike grabbed the plungers for the claymores 50 yards away and began setting them off. He still had the burn mark from changing out the barrel on the M60. All this time, thousands of AK 47s are firing at him. As he was setting off the claymores, a mortar landed five yards from the bunker. One buddy was only recognizable because he had a peace bracelet on. Mike told me how he watched the blood drain from his other buddy who had a big piece of shrapnel protruding from his chest.

Mike didn't have a scratch on him, but he lost most of the hearing in his ear. He grabbed the horn and first called in artillery danger close. Just as he was calling it, the other bunker took a direct hit. They were all dead.

"The last two guys with me said, we gotta Evac now! I told them to get back to the (command) bunker. I watched them climb out and both got clipped as soon they stood up. I knew I was dead so I was going to take as many out as I could. The air smelled like blood. I will never get over the smell of war. I grabbed the horn and called Broken Arrow." That's when an American company is about to be overrun and calls in all air support.

"If I was going to die, I'd rather my brothers kill me."

I was hearing things his wife never heard. I knew what Esprit de Corp was at that moment.

"There were a bunch of Vietnamese soldiers fighting with us in Vietnam." Mike continued, calmly smoking a cigarette as he purged this nightmare. "I knew the Sandies (close air support aircraft) were on the way and stacks more (planes) above. It took about a minute for the howitzers to adjust. They were aiming 50 yards out and walking it in. When I heard the thumps two clicks out, I jumped out on the left side of the bunker and I saw one of the Vietnamese guys who was with us running towards the bunker with a pack on his back. I was running for my life because I knew what was coming and I didn't know if he was a secret VC going to blow the command bunker or what. Something just wasn't right. So, I took my 45 and shot him in the head."

By the time the sun came up, the Marines had dropped over 1,000 rounds of 155mm artillery shells. The Air Force had destroyed all the vegetation surrounding the command bunker and dropped enough napalm to scorch the surrounding area. When Mike came back and landed in San Diego, a Christian preacher was there to greet the soldiers.

"Have you accepted the Lord Jesus Christ as your Lord and Savior?"

"No, I haven't."

"Well my child, you must, or your everlasting soul will go to hell."

"I've already been there."

My friend Mike is dead.

He tried to drown those memories with alcohol. More than you can possibly imagine. We were playing pool one day and we got to talking about Mohammed Ali. My mom was an art teacher and she and her students painted a mural on the wall of Martin Luther King elementary school of Ali. Ali came to the dedication and took pictures with the kids.

"I love Ali. He was the only black guy who really stuck it to the racists and Nixon who survived. He was right about everything. I didn't go there for freedom or anything else those lying bastards said. My buddies didn't die for their country. They died because a bunch of rich white men always send off the poor white trash to die in wars they can profit from. That's the lie they tell to seduce us into surrendering our lives. It's the way it's always been and always will be. Ali got that.

'Why should they ask me to put on a uniform and go ten thousand miles from home and drop bombs and bullets on brown people in Vietnam while so-called Negro people in Louisville are treated like dogs and denied simple human rights? No, I am not going ten thousand miles from home to help murder and burn another poor nation simply to continue the domination of white slave masters of the darker people the world over. This is the day when such evils must come to an end. I have been warned that to take such a stand would put my prestige in jeopardy and could cause me to lose millions of dollars which should accrue to me as the champion. But I have said it once and I will say it again. The real enemy of my people is right here. I will not disgrace my religion, my people or myself by becoming a tool to enslave those who are fighting for their own justice, freedom and equality… If I thought the war was going to bring freedom and equality to 22 million of my people, they wouldn't have to draft me, I'd join tomorrow. But I either have to obey the laws of the land or the laws of Allah. I have nothing to lose by standing up for my beliefs. So I'll go to jail. We've been in jail for four hundred years.'

I'm not a sports fan. I especially don't like football because it is a brutal game that causes brain damage in athletes. Science is bringing the consequences that football does to light. The NFL tried covering up the head trauma damage football does to its athletes.

But there are bigger moral issues for me that I am just not comfortable being silent about anymore. The NFL enjoys a special status in the US where they are granted a monopoly by our government and they are granted an absurd 'non-profit' status the same as most charities and churches enjoy. Only in this 'charity', the beneficiaries are not the people who build these obscene stadiums for billionaire owners who are not accountable at all to the people who pay for them, whether they want to or not.

That level of unbridled greed should fill most of these geriatric white men insane with glee but of course it doesn't. These men are not merely content to profit from the labor of black men, tax-free no less. No, they also want to tell them whether they can kneel in silent protest to the summary executions that white police officers are giving to unarmed black men.

In the NFL, you can beat your girlfriend or wife and not even raise an eyebrow. You can use performance enhancing drugs and that's no big deal. You can rape women and well, that's not acceptable but you can still play. But kneeling during the national anthem? Well, that'll get you death threats and thrown out of the league if you're black.

That is most decidedly entirely un-American. Protests in all forms are not just patriotic, they are as American as apple pie. Colin Kaepernick's silent protest was never about the flag or veterans or anything but protesting injustice. For too long we have ignored the voices of people of color and dismissed them as sour grape complaints or for Colin, whining from a privileged millionaire. Anyone who says such a bloody horrible thing is not only a racist, but they do not understand that he is using his privilege to try to right a wrong we as white people are responsible for because we will not see this wrong and lift a finger to right it.

A lot of people burned their Nike shoes because Nike hired Colin to be part of their ad campaign. They're the same people who tried to put Ali in jail and spat on him, sent him death threats and called him a 'Ni**er traitor.' We have a shameful history of racism in this country and whenever they see an 'uppity' black man making them uncomfortable, they first question his patriotism and it is simply shocking how many of these hatriots have never done a damn thing for freedom but are so keen to deny the rights of a Colin Kaepernick the same way they did to Mohammed Ali.

The shortest poem in the English language doesn't have much meaning to such people who burn shoes instead of crosses. What it misses is context, history and the dignity of the Greatest Boxer there ever was. He was that to be sure, but when he said it aloud, the gravitas begins to seep in, and it still makes the hair on the back of my neck stand up because I can see the beauty and the gravity of a man who was on the right side of history in the same way Colin Kaepernick was.

"I, we."

- Mohammed Ali

## Dean

English was always my worst subject. I loved to read but I couldn't get the words to come out right. I had terrible headaches starting at 13 because I had a brain tumor wrapped around my optic nerve, although I didn't find that out until I was 30.

I had to get a tooth pulled and the dentist gave me some Tylenol 3 with codeine for the pain which I had no intention ever of taking. One night, I was 15, I was having one of my headaches and I thought, 'well let's try some of these and see what happens.'

The best way I can describe my brain when I learn something, is that it's like a switch being flicked on. One day at lunch, I looked up at the window when a storm was moving in and I saw this oddly shaped cloud and I imagined the equations on that cloud and a switch went on and it just made sense to me.

When the codeine kicked in, it was like a switch clicked on and I started writing. I wrote and wrote all week. The levee broke.

Sophomore year I had Dean Robertson as my English teacher. She scared the shit out of me. First, because her homework assignments were enough to keep even the best students up all night and they did. Apparently, it never occurred to her or the other teachers that we needed sleep and the other teachers were entirely oblivious to the fact that they too were assigning enough homework to also keep us up all night.

She would say, 'well they're not going to let you get away with that when you get to college.' When I got in my first English class in college, it was like falling into a gossamer blanket while being surrounded by kittens.

Dean has a commanding presence. She could intimidate rare geniuses with her high-powered intellect. I was so afraid to go into her class because woe to anyone who arose one of her contemptible scowls which struck a kind of terror that would make any man beg for emasculation.

Many described her as a feminist zealot to be reckoned with, which was true. Male students speculated that she hated men because of her militant lesbianism. Some of these idiots didn't know we were going to school with her son.

The thing was, I wanted to please her. Even then I knew that the tough exterior was there to protect the soft interior. Those who have experienced the slings and arrows of outrageous fortune can see the wounded no matter how well they conceal their scars.

One day, I was living in an efficiency apartment in an old school with a bunch of convicted child molesters. I thought about how Dean had a poster of Emily Dickinson in her classroom and I wanted to know what she was about. I had just finished the Norton's Anthology of English Literature 2nd edition, so I was familiar with the poets. I went to the Jeffersonville Library -a fabulous library, incidentally- and checked out her complete works. Needless to say, Emily blew my mind. She was a tour de force. She opened my mind to nuances I would never have known as a man.

Dean is one of those teachers who changed me profoundly as a human being and I want her to know it, along with all of you.

### Shania Twain

I was in a bit of a pickle if I'm honest.

You see, the way I was brought up, I had one older sister and two behind, and a mother who was somewhere between a Category 5 hurricane and a thermonuclear device. And believe you me, every one of those sisters had Mom's attitude when the occasion arose.

Upstairs we had five bedrooms, a laundry room, and the library. Mom had her own bathroom in the master. The older one and one right behind me shared a bathroom and the youngest wanted her own downstairs. Now if you were to look at the door on that shared bathroom you would have to conclude that whatever dogs were in that fight couldn't have survived. But there it was.

For some reason at one time, Cathy required an ax to get her door open. I don't know the specifics, but Lesli had gone past her time allotment, apparently. I never understood why they couldn't use Mom's bathroom or one of the others, but I can assure you that Cathy whacked that door with that ax. Sadly, it did not help her gain entry. She hadn't mastered physics or the art of proper ax handling yet, but she would.

Meanwhile, I was figuring out that physical violence was a bad option. I might have won a temporary battle against one of them, but I would have lost the war against all three. My sisters believed in a scorched earth policy in even the smallest conflict. I learned early that I was a man and woefully stupid compared to the hive. So for instance, when my sisters failed to do their chores at Dad's house, it always seemed to be entirely my fault. To this day, I don't know how they managed that, only that they managed it with 100% success for as long as we were all going to Dad's.

When trying to achieve a modicum of justice, an adolescent male must do two things: outsmart the women and protect the family jewels from the broad foot of an angry sister. So justice was no small matter. Sun Tsu had very good advice when he said,

"Whenever possible get your enemies to fight each other."

To accomplish this you can, for instance, remove all the toilet paper from the girls' bathroom. Their first inclination will be to blame each other, and mayhem is certain to follow. As the righteous one, you can feign innocence. Try saying over your shoulder as you pass them in the hall:

"As if I care about what happens in your disgusting bathroom."

Another technique for inducing bloodlust is to dump a new bottle of a favorite shampoo down the drain. The owner will naturally believe it is the other's federal offense and fisticuffs are imminent. My point is that when outnumbered four to one, it's best to use your brains and protect the gonads.

I was married when a series of unfortunate events transpired. It was about three years after my brain tumor surgery, and I had bought a Lexus SC 400 - still my favorite car. It was black with coach leather seats, and it just looked awesome. On Sundays, I liked to wash it, breaking out the Zymol once a month and waxing it up perfect. It had a Nakamichi stereo system, and I had lost about 50% of my hearing from the tumor.

My next-door neighbor was a stay-at-home mom. She had a big Nissan 4x4 with the "Baby on Board" thing mounted on her rear window. The husband looked like a guy who worked all the time. I am telling you one thing, if potted plants were an art, she was the Michelangelo of them. Her front entrance looked like an opening to another dimension, one made entirely of flowers. Her back deck--above and below--was like a shot out of the Victory Garden. I'll go out on a limb here and say I saw the signs of an obsession. It was a bit strange since there were no trees in our little subdivision to help with any shade-loving flowers, but I can tell you, she was good.

It took me about two years to recover from the surgery and washing the car was physically difficult for me. My Sunday routine was all about the car. For the neighbors it was church. They'd come home from what seemed to me an awfully long time to spend in church and I'd nod to the hubby. Michelangelo never looked at me. And that's how it was at my end of the street, week in and week out. Never changed.

I think my parents secretly hoped that one day I would develop the patience and tolerance to just let it slide when people behave rudely. I hated to disappoint them, but hey there you are.

So this one day, I was out waxing the car, listening to the Smashing Pumpkins and the Mrs. comes home from church alone. Her hubby was often gone, so I didn't think anything about it. About ten minutes later, my friendly neighborhood police officer pulled in for a chat.

My general attitude about police officers is definitely not good, and being the son and grandson of the most powerful lawyers in the state has made it worse. So I can come to a boil real fast when officers ain't acting with civility and good manners. When you are introducing yourself in the South, it's best to use pleasantries to demonstrate you are worthy of civility. Good manners dictate that a man be a gentleman at all times while visiting on another man's property.

"What are you doing out here?" is not an acceptable greeting for a gentleman or a police officer, especially with towels and soapy buckets about with sponges and such floating in them.

Clearly this ruffian was not only rude and un-gentlemanly, he seemed to be lacking the connection between his eyes and his brain as he was unable to register a car, a person, and car-washing paraphernalia and deduce that I was washing my car in my driveway. He also did not offer his hand which is yet another etiquette violation of the egregious order. I knew that there was a high probability that he was afflicted with some manner of nincompoopery. I addressed him accordingly.

"Well it may come as a shock to you, Einstein, but I am waxing my car."

I don't know if it was because Einstein was a Jew or because he was a genius, but my policeman friend definitely didn't like me calling him Einstein at all. I did that on purpose, knowing that it is important to let a public servant know that he is there to serve by using a vernacular above his education level. Put him in his place right out of the gate, so to speak. I could pretty much count on him not recognizing irony.

"I need your name and ID."

This was a familiar scene that had been played out many thousands of times with my dad and his brothers. I always paid attention when they were discussing the dumbest cops they encountered on the witness stand, so I was more than prepared to respond to this fatuous ignoramus' query.

"You can call me Sir, and no you may not have my ID."

It's important to maintain a position of dominance over all cops lest they become aggressive, as I could tell this one was about to do. It's also worth mentioning that if the guy had just been polite it would have already ended this unnecessary interaction, but cops aren't trained to de-escalate anything.

"Well we got a noise complaint, so I am going to need you to turn down your radio."

Apparently, he was unaware that noise has to be above 100 decibels and past 9:00 at night to be considered a violation. What was more perturbing to me was that somebody didn't appreciate my excellent selection of tunes being broadcast free of charge. Ah, there was the rub. There was a Shania Twain fan nearby.

"I'll take your suggestion under advisement thanks. Have a nice day."

Just a note here. They are always confused by phrases like "under advisement." This guy didn't know what it meant, but I'll bet he'd heard it in court or somewhere else he'd looked stupid.

That should have been the end of it, but this cop was a spry lad wholly unaware that I was the progeny of the attorney currently representing the chief of police in his d-i-v-o-r-c-e.

"You can either turn down your radio or you can go to jail."

"Excuse me for just a moment while I consult with my legal counsel."

I called the old man.

"Dad, I'm here with Officer Sweatyballs and he is insisting that I turn down my radio. He mentioned 6th and Jefferson. (the jail)

"Gimme just a sec."

"Just another minute Officer Sweatyballs. He's consulting his law books and such."

About one minute later, Officer Sweatyballs' cell phone began ringing. I heard a couple of 'yes sirs' and 'very good sirs,' and then Officer Sweatyballs said,

"I apologize for disturbing you Mr. Clay. It won't happen again."

Sundays the old man likes to fire up his grill and cook chicken and ribs for his friends. It turned out that when Dad answered the phone, he put me on speaker and well, guess what? Apparently, the Chief of the Police was sitting right next to him enjoying one of those German pilsners he likes to drink. So he called up dispatch and had them put Officer Sweatyballs on the phone so the Chief could tell him about his new nightshift assignment. Dad being the famous cross-examiner that he is, he also inquired who it was that made the call.

I had found the Shania Twain fan and let's just say, she didn't impress me much.

I chalked this misdemeanor offense up to me being a tad deaf and didn't think any more about it, until two Sundays later when she did it again. It turned out that her hubby was in Saudi Arabia working for some shipping company and he was gone for six weeks and Shania needed something to do. Mind you that if she had just come out and told me that the Metallica was disturbing her, it would have been my duty as a gentleman of the South to honor her request. I concluded that she had come from some Yankee hovel above the Mason-Dixon. Like the officer, she didn't understand the power of good manners.

The next officer who came to chide me about my Metallica concert stopped in the street. I saw him on his radio fiddling about. I fully expected another query into my music selection, but I was wrong.

"Good afternoon Mr. Clay. I just wanted to shake hands with you because your dad helped an amigo of mine out and he's the best. I just wanted to tell you that you might want to make peace with your neighbor because she don't like you too much."

"Thanks Officer Ortiz. I appreciate you."

I had a sneaking suspicion that he had heard about Officer Sweatyballs.

"In case you don't know, Sweatyballs is on third shift now." He laughed.

In High School, there was a guy named William who liked to talk to a plant in biology class. He was trying to make sure it had all the carbon dioxide it could use. Apparently, this was annoying to people who did not enjoy listening to William nattering on with his plant endlessly.

Our Chemistry teacher was a living Cruella DeVille. As if that weren't enough, she was a Rhodes Scholar and a man-hating lesbian who passed out disciplinary reports like Dalmatian hides. She was especially demonic about the cleaning of test tubes. We were only allowed to use her favorite product, Alconox. It comes in a cardboard milk container and it's a bunch of small balls that look like Styrofoam.

Suppose you put three tiny balls of Alconox into your washing machine and turn it on. Within minutes, there would be enough foam to fill your entire house and any nearby skyscraper. It is the most extreme base and if you got it on your clothes, it would bleach them. I'm with Cruella on this. It is the greatest detergent ever made.

So one day, someone asked Cruella what she thought was the best way to kill vegetation? Without thinking what was being asked of her she innocently said, "Change the Ph levels of the dirt."

That person got a couple of beads of Alconox and proceeded to "treat" William's plant with a lethal dose. William naturally thought he wasn't watering it enough as it began its journey into death. He was at the point of hysteria as all of his efforts failed to revive his plant from its grave.

This was the second time Shania had called the popo on yours truly and breached the traditions of etiquette that generally keep us from killing each other. It was time that she learned a few things about being a good neighbor and I was just the one to teach her.

I'll risk raising a potentially hot topic just to say that a person with a murderous rage and a long garden hose is perhaps not someone you'd pick to seal your plant's doom, but Shania was obviously not a MENSA member.

I was going to need another 50 feet of garden hose. Amazingly you can order Alconox online and have it overnighted. I didn't need a half gallon of it, but it was on sale and I could use the left over to wash my car. I hit Walmart for the hose. As I got to the garden section, there was actually a very respectable choice of herbicides and one included a complimentary spray attachment that I could put to good use.

Our subdivision House Association was extremely anal about mowing the grass, maintaining bushes and if I had ever bothered to go to one of the meetings, I might have seen Mrs. Shania Victory Garden getting an award for the prettiest lawn/garden in the entire subdivision.

I don't know what reaction I was expecting between the Alconox and the vegetation killer but as I was mixing it up I swear I saw a cartoon skull and bones floating out of it. I had also managed to procure a nearly silent electric power washer to effect maximum damage and not cross onto my victim's property.

The moon was full at one o'clock on the night I began executing the Victory Garden's doom. It looked like it was snowing soap. I slathered the plants with Alconox as I cackled with murderous glee. All her work toiling in the spring was for naught. I couldn't hit the top of her deck with the normal hose, so the pressure washer did just the trick.

I sprayed the sod they had bought to look absolutely perfect for the Homeowners Association with a thick layer. Chernobyl couldn't do the damage I was doing. I stared at two bunny rabbits eying me like I was committing a war crime, which I was because snitches get stitches, bitches. I even soaked the evergreens because I wanted to taste her complete meltdown when it came. I wanted to see those fucking Housing Association warnings strewn across her former lawn like toppled gravestones. I wanted everyone to drive by and wonder how her victory garden had turned into the barren Superfund wasteland I was turning it into while whistling the theme music to Andy Griffith's show!

I didn't tell my wife about it but being a chemist herself, she did ask me what happened to the new bottle of Alconox.

She'd see soon enough.

On the fourth day, Shania knew something was badly wrong. She was dumping water on her potted plants like they had been stuck in sub-Saharan Africa in the middle of summer. I watched out my window while she spread the Alconox deeper into the roots. They weren't looking good, but she still tried to save them. The grass first lost whatever causes it to stand up. It fell over like a worn shag carpet. It was dead. On the day the hubby was home, he bought a splitter for his garden hose so he could run his sprayers 24 hours. I heard him ask Shania why the soil was so soapy?

On the tenth day, the evergreens turned brown. If you stood where their grass was, it would peel off like dead flesh and you would slip in the mud that was their former front yard. The hubby just ran the sprinklers day and night with a futility that only I could enjoy. All of her potted plants were dead. They'd need a backhoe to get the evergreens out. I saw her pleading with the Homeowner's Association.

Clearly, I was the suspect.

On the sixteenth day, a Detective from the Kentucky State Troopers came by for a chat. He knocked on the door. He was wearing a Trooper blazer with his badge dangling out of the pocket. He had damning pictures of dead plants and a lawn destroyed by clearly alien forces. He wanted answers damnit. This sweet Christian lady had been violated. Nobody could get her to stop crying. He was none too impressed with the petulant son of the famous lawyer.

"Come in detective. Can I pour you a cup of fresh coffee? I have some cheese Danishes that are the best things ever."

I could tell he wanted them because he paused for a moment, but he wasn't there for a social call. He had questions. I had a cigarette box on the table and pointed to those. He did take one. I lit it.

" Mr. Clay, I am here because of some unfortunate reasons regarding your neighbors."

"Oh? How can I help?"

" Well if you hadn't noticed, they're having some issues with their grass and lawn."

"No kidding? Maybe they should consult with a landscape architect. I'm all thumbs when it comes to botany."

"Well Mr. Clay, she thinks maybe there was some foul play involved with her lawn issues and that you're the cause of all the problems."

By this time, my wife was in tears. She was crying rivers. I believe to this day that the detective thought these were tears of innocence but no, she was trying to control her laughter and knowledge of the crime. This is the funniest thing in history.

"Why would she possibly think that?" I asked, innocently.

"Well, she said a while back you were blasting music and she called the police to get you to turn it down. "

"Oh I remember now. That was her? I thought it was the ones across the street. They seem a bit shady to me."

" Shady how?"

"Well I don't mean to tell tales out of school, but I do believe they are marijuana smokers." I said, as my wife made an excuse to leave the room before she blew my cover with her hysterical laughter.

"I do have a bit of a hearing problem," I continued. "I had a brain tumor a while back and so I don't hear so good, but I know I'm not over 100 decibels."

" Well there was another incident where she called the police about your playing the music too loud."

"No kidding? I don't recall any other instances off hand. Besides, how would I have known it was even her that called?"

" Well, I seen who your daddy is and thought he mighta found out for you."

"I don't have one hint." (but you're welcome to question the chief of police until kingdom come if you like jag off)

" The thing is, in this picture here, you can see that it looks like someone has dripped something on your grass and killed it as well. Just like what happened to your neighbor."

A fucking couple of Alconox drops had betrayed me!

"I guess I'll need to get my soil tested in case it's contagious huh?"

He was whipped, battered, destroyed, bamboozled and he knew it. Sadly for Shania's victory garden, murdering foliage is not a crime. He gathered up his pictures.

" I guess I'll tell her she ought not call the police over petty things."

I grabbed his hand and shook it firmly.

"That's sage advice detective," I said with a wink.

## Nicole

When I was in Benidorm on the Costa Blanca in Spain, I was going through a bit of culture shock at seeing bare-breasted women for the first time. There was one particular specimen that really was so grand, that in a just world, all straight men and every lesbian within sight would have stood and applauded. She was movie-star gorgeous.

My friend Alex just walked up to her and asked her if she would like to have some tapas with us. She said something in French, which luckily Alex knew. He spoke five languages. He was Russian and did not give a fuck that she was the most beautiful woman on the planet. She agreed and proceeded to cover her gloriously large, round, supple breasts.

Her name was Nicole.

She smelled like that heavenly suntan oil all over her tanned body.

We go to this bar and it's holy week in Europe which is spring break here. There are just thousands of people everywhere and as we're walking to the bar, Nicole is stopping traffic with every man in sight catcalling her and all that. She and Alex are chatting up a storm in French when Alex gestures toward me and says something something French 'Tomas'.

'Oh you're American?' she purred in perfect English.

I nearly passed out that she was talking to me.

There were about ten of us and our drinks and tapas arrive and we sit down at a table. So you understand, I've spent every waking hour with these guys for three weeks and not one of them speaks a lick of English. Even Alex. The night I got there, we went into a bowling alley with my trusty English/Spanish dictionary and I glance at it and look up a few words and they say in Spanish, "Oh that must be a Mexican dictionary. We don't know what that means.' So after about four tries, I throw the damn dictionary in the garbage. They did miraculously know the lyrics to Bon Jovi songs, only they were fucking awful. It sounded like, 'chot tu ta har an tor tu game`darren tu gib lub a baa name.'

So here I am at a table with the most spectacular specimen of the opposite sex trying to keep my jaw attached to my skull and Alex suggests that I tell Nicole a joke.

"Yes, yes please do Tomas."

Like I could possibly say no to her.

"Four nuns die and arrive at the gates of heaven. Saint Peter is there and asks the first nun if she had ever touched a penis.

'Yes,' she admits. "I once touched a penis with the tip of my finger.,

'Dip your finger into the holy water and enter the kingdom of Heaven,' says Saint Peter. The nun dips her finger in the holy water and enters heaven.

Saint Peter asks the same question of the second nun. 'Yes,' she admits. 'I once touched a penis with one hand.'

'Dip your hand into the holy water and enter the kingdom of Heaven,' says Saint Peter. The second nun complies and enters heaven.

At this point, the fourth nun abruptly cuts in line.

'Hang on!' she says, pointing at the third nun. 'You'd better let me go next because there's no way I'm gargling that shit after she sticks her ass in it!'"

I'm staring Nicole dead in her beautiful blue eyes. She erupts in laughter. But there is a strange sound coming from the gallery of my friends. I turn and look at these miserable rotten Judas Iscariot motherfuckers and they are slapping their hands on the table! Thippi is literally crying. David has fallen on the ground. Alex is doubled over because every single one of these miserable bastards not only speaks English, they're as fluent as I am!

Apparently, they were under the strictest orders from my Aunt Betsy to not utter a word of English to me while I was there and finally the jig was up and every single one of them was going to pay in blood for fucking with me! This, of course, launched them into a tsunami of laughter as I smacked each one of these bastards upside the head! Snot and tears were coming out of all of us we were laughing so hard.

I explain to Nicole the treachery she has just witnessed. She found it entertaining, to say the least. The ladies get up and go to the bathroom. I am about two sheets to the wind and as they come back through the bar, they had to pass through a gauntlet of men. I'm watching Nicole navigate the gauntlet when she turns and smacks this guy.

Alex was about 6'3" and maybe 230 pounds. He could handle his booze - having a Russian liver and all. He had gold chains on his neck and he had to shave twice a day because his beard grew that much. He suddenly became an Olympic long jumper as he leaped out of his seat, picked up this grab-assing bitch by the neck, and carried him over to Nicole, who was clearly upset.

"Please Nicole, address this thing in any way you like."

She began slapping him in what can only be described as a French conniption fit. This went on for maybe 2 minutes and then the other women had a turn slapping him as much as they liked.

David torqued him down to his knees.

"And what would you like to say to these ladies?"

I don't know what he said exactly but believe me, he was all kinds of sorry. The cops had come by then and they just stood by as David administered some street justice. Then he disappeared into the night, arm in arm with the cops.

It was one of the best nights of my life. For years afterward, I used to dream about Nicole and what it would be like to wake up next to a woman like that after a night of unbridled passion. Surely nothing ever could be better. Until I thought of something that might equal it.

Watching any Trump doing a perp walk.

### Rachmaninoff

If you ever make it to the Smithsonian, there's a strangely small room on one of the corners that has probably $50 million worth of Stradivarius masterpieces. I remember thinking that all one would have to do is smash a glass case and walk out with several of them. When mom and I got there, someone was playing one of the cellos. I asked if I could touch it. The woman playing it was maybe 60 and she obliged me.

We were going to look at the Hope diamond. Something about diamonds stirs something in a lot of women. Mom was one of those types.

They had a replica of the Hope Diamond that was $80. Mom looked at and I could tell she wanted it, but she wouldn't spend that much for it. When she scooted down to look around the display cases, I slipped my card to the cashier and got it for her. I dropped in my back pocket and we rounded the corner which went back towards the music section.

We walked in and there were a bunch of plaster hands on display. Something drew me to these ones that were really large. Bigger than my hands anyway and I wear an XL glove. The woman who was playing the cello saw me looking at them earnestly and asked me if I'd like to touch them? 'Just those ones,' I said. She opened up the case and pulled them out.

I knew they were from the master, the virtuoso of virtuosos, Rachmaninoff. His hands were at least a XXXL. Long powerful fingers. You kind of imagine that you're touching his actual hands when you touch the casts. I thought to myself, 'so that's what it takes to play the rack 3.'

It's hard to describe the subtle nuances of one particular virtuoso. If you listen enough to Horowitz play Beethoven, you know when he plays versus someone else. Horowitz had very light fingers. Rachmaninoff does not. He pounds the keys with passion and fury. If you know the rack 3, you know only a virtuoso can play it. It is one of, if not the most difficult piano concertos to play.

Music means different things to everyone. One song can take you back to your youth. When you first had a song you shared with someone else and it was your song and it meant something intimate that only you two knew about. Mom was doing chemo at the National Cancer Institute when the movie Shine came out. I remember going to see it the Saturday night before Mother's Day. We went to this nice seafood place right on the water in Baltimore near the Orioles Stadium. We had the blue crab cakes and they are still the best I can remember... yes, better than the ones in Boston.

I slipped mom the hope diamond replica. She saw it and just lit up like a Christmas tree. Mom would walk around in jeans and a flannel shirt with a hope diamond replica pinned on it and carry $10,000 in hundred-dollar bills in a gangster roll.

"Let people get the wrong impression of you. It sorts out the riff raff you don't want around you anyway."

Every year on Mother's Day, I listen to the rack 3 and spill a few tears because that's what it means to me. Go look up a performance of it by Olga Kern. It literally takes my breath away.

Her hands are small but mighty, just like my mom's.

## Best Drugs Ever

After my brain surgery, I had the best drugs ever. My pain doctor was also a lawyer and by then, the LMPD had caused two other physicians to commit suicide. They tried to intimidate my doctor but that didn't work. One of the suicides was a cancer doctor who got turned into "Dr. Oxycontin." They arrested him at his office and suspended his prescription privileges. 8 of his patients committed suicide.

The police officers in the Louisville Metro Narcotics Unit used the KASPER report (as in Casper the friendly ghost) to see who was prescribing the most narcotics. They then went to these doctors and tried to get them to write prescriptions for ailments the detectives faked. After the 2nd suicide, the police spokeswoman said, "if he weren't guilty, he wouldn't have done that." He happened to be a decorated Vietnam surgeon who got a pain management specialty when he got back to help the men who he had treated in country who were maimed.

In 1968, Nixon told John Erlichman and John Mitchell that they needed to devise a way to take care of political enemies.

What he meant was to control black people. The only thing that they wanted to control was their ability to vote. So they came up with the Controlled Substances Act of 1969. That was the beginning of the drug war that continues to this day. John Mitchell is the only Attorney General convicted of felonies and sent to prison.

Not only did this evil law spawn the prison industrial complex, it began 50 years of injustice across the globe. We sprayed Dioxin all over Southeast Asia and South America trying to eradicate poppy and coca fields. Dioxin is also known as "Agent Orange." It causes all types of cancers, but it also causes horrible birth defects.

Felons naturally cannot vote, and we have decimated black families for half a century by treating drug addiction as a crime problem instead of a public health problem.

"Get tough on criminals" is really a good talking point if you're a politician because who isn't against criminals? It's also something that appeals to simple minds who don't think about spending millions of dollars on an ounce of marijuana. Convict someone under the 3-strike law and they get 25 to life. 25 years times $40k a year is a million dollars.

There's an additional cost to continuing Nixon's evil war.

April 21, 2016 will forever be the anniversary of Prince Rogers Nelson's death. The police decided there would be no further prosecutions in his case. He died of an opioid overdose. Where he was getting his fentanyl is not known. What is known is that he was not getting it from his doctor. Prince was suffering from a back injury and he could not find a doctor who could treat his pain effectively, so he sought it through other means.

Instead of a doctor helping him, he got some street dealer supply it and it killed him. By any measure, Prince was a rare genius. Phillip Seymour Hoffman overdosed. Heath Ledger overdosed. Michael Jackson overdosed. Whitney Houston overdosed. Amy Winehouse, Chris Farley, John Belushi, River Phoenix, Janis Joplin, Jim Morrison, Jimi Hendrix, Scott Weiland, Tom Petty, Elvis Presley and so many others died from drug abuse.

We have spent over a trillion dollars on this evil war. We've made a bunch of high school graduates who know nothing about medicine to determine the quality of life of sick people who they firmly believe are disposable.

We have got to do something else because this evil war is doing more damage to Americans than ISIS ever dreamed of. We don't need to cut funding to the arts or education, we need to cut funding to the DEA entirely. If you want to do something about this, change your thinking.

The life you save just might be your own.

Dr. Everything'll Be Alright

Make everything go wrong

Pills and thrills and daffodils will kill

Hang tough children

## Pop's Toolbox

Pop had this wooden toolbox he made. He took it everywhere when he had to go to Florida, Michigan or Oklahoma. When I was about 14, he took me out to the garage and opened it up and started pulling out everything. When he got to the bottom, he had these two long metal hooks that sprung a lock at the bottom. At the bottom there were two hammers and two saws.

"Do you know what those are, son?" He always called me son.

I knew better than to answer: "two hammers and two saws."

"We were so poor that my daddy would take me to any house that burned down just so we could get the nails. These are all that's left of my daddy."

One of the hammers was really unusual because it had two claws on it. I had never seen one like that. A few years later I saw an Antique Roadshow that had a guy who brought in some tools. The special was a double claw hammer just like the one Pop showed me. They estimated it at $50,000. It sold at auction for $155,000.

He wanted me to keep them safe. Nobody else knew they were there. My sisters sold his toolbox at a yard sale.

It's one of the many reasons they are all dead to me.

My mother hated my Uncle Chuck. He was a grabasser. My mom was a very beautiful woman. She endured a lot of men putting their hands on her until she got out of college. Her first husband was a pro basketball player. She said, "those sons of bitches didn't touch me when I got married." I shudder to think of the beating I would get if I had ever touched a woman like that.

I think a lot of it is a generational thing. There were a lot of TV shows and Movies where men would smack a woman on the ass or grope them in some way. They're dying now.

I'm 48 years old now and I've seen three sea changes. The one complete reversal was marriage equality and the tormenting of LGBTQ people becoming taboo.

Racism, too is becoming more taboo and when most of the Baby boomers die in the next ten years, it will become very taboo.

What is perhaps the quickest sea change is the #metoo movement that is dredging up these old clods who think they can do whatever they want or have done whatever they've wanted, and are now paying the price. I personally don't give a damn how many of these fuckers go down. The more the better.

I remember when Chuck died, Pop told me that he finally accepted Jesus as his savior and he went to heaven. I thought: "well fuck, I can live the most hateful and immoral life and just ask for clemency and get it? What a bunch of shit." That's the scam these evangelical hucksters are running. Hypocrisy always leaves a bad taste in my mouth.

I miss Pop a bunch.

## Spain

If you ask a smoker who the most intolerable people are to be around, it's a reformed smoker. Know why? Because we won't listen to your bullshit cognitive dissonance since we've already slain that demon.

You know what is the most intolerable thing for a racist? A reformed racist.

When I was 17, dad sent me to Spain to visit with my Aunt Betsy. I was ten when she found out this Spaniard she met down in Miami was going to get married and well, she weren't going to let some Spanish hussy steal her man. So she got on an airplane and went to Spain. She packed a suitcase and left all of her belongings behind. We had to go pick up everything she left behind and bring it back here. She's been married to the kindest man I've ever met ever since.

Jose had some kind of birth defect in his ear and it gave him hyper-sensitive hearing. He was already a famous sound engineer in Spain. He had pictures of himself with Mick and

Keith, U2, Bowie, Freddie and a bunch more. When I was there, he was recording with the Psychedelic Furs.

When you travel to another country, you instantly understand what Mark Twain meant when he said: "Travel is fatal to prejudice, bigotry, and narrow-mindedness, and many of our people need it sorely on these accounts. Broad, wholesome, charitable views of men and things cannot be acquired by vegetating in one little corner of the earth all one's lifetime."

Right next to the Prado Museum in Madrid is Retiro Park. Betsy had a friend named Ann who was showing me the sights. She had a full mane of grey hair and she was the most beautiful woman I had been in the presence of. Think Kim Bassinger in 9 1/2 weeks. We were sitting on a bench, enjoying the spectacular view and I see a gorgeous woman walking with a dapper black guy. He stopped and pulled her hand gently and spun her to him and began kissing her passionately.

I'm from Kentucky and though Jefferson Davis was from the Bluegrass State, we fought for the Union in what the rebels call, even today, 'the war of northern aggression.' Anything below the Mason Dixon line is considered the south and we have a certain "heritage" that still flows in the veins of descendants of the Civil War.

Now anyone from the South knows exactly what I am saying without saying it explicitly. What I just said there is a not-so-secret code spoken among white people like a wink wink nod nod that I too am racist and it's okay to speak freely. When I was young and ignorant as can be, I didn't see any harm in it because everyone I knew was like that.

I'd never seen a black man kiss a white woman before. I felt like I was walking through some mind-bending universe seeing every masterpiece the Prado had and buildings hundreds of years old on a splendid day. I was sitting with the most beautiful woman I had ever seen and my initial feeling of discomfort witnessing this private moment turned to utter fascination because she was smiling and laughing as he dipped and twirled her round. I looked at Ann and wished I had the nerve to do the same with her. He was singing as he walked away. I said to Ann, "so that's what it's like to be gaga in love."

To this day, it still makes me smile.

I sat up that night still reeling from jet lag and I began putting every racist I knew on a grid in my mind. Then I began recognizing their patterns and similarities and the first thing I noticed was they were all stupid. I'm talking dumb as stumps. Then I said to myself, 'They haven't been to Spain either.' I just didn't want to be like *them* anymore. I was never like them anyway. They let me know every single time I used my 'fancy college words.'

I still follow my hometown newspaper the Courier Journal. When Nike announced that Colin Kaepernick was going to be their spokesperson for the 30th anniversary of the Just Do It campaign, they had a post about it and like a dog returneth to his vomit, I had to look. It was a horror show of white people livid at Nike for their villainous miscegenation by employing that 'anti-American N.....,' I mean black man. You see, in the south and most of America, if you're black, you ain't 'sposed to protest freedom when we let you be a millionaire playing in the NFL.

KNOW YOUR PLACE YOU BLACK SON OF A BITCH!

Well let me tell all you Bubbas and Tammy Lynns out there, having 'a black friend' does not inoculate you from being racist. When you get home and start burning your Nike gear to protest Colin, it proves you are racists. ALL of you need to do some deep soul-searching because Colin and everyone else who looks like him don't have a problem. You do. And I'll be goddamned if you think I am going to see all the injustice my black brothers and sisters have to suffer because of your dumb asses and stay silent about it!

If you want to be something more than the rot on our society, then stop saying you aren't racist just because you don't say ni**er no more. If you don't want to be called racist, then stop voting racists into office and start making the world a better place where everything isn't about putting the dumbest person possible in charge. If you're pissed off about a black man protesting the summary executions of unarmed black people then you are a dyed-in-the-wool Yee Hawing racist and I am tired of you embarrassing the country because you lack the courage to sever the chains of racism which were put on you by your parents.

You're missing so much more beauty in your life that the chains of racism rob you of. Believe me I know, I used to be just like you, then I went to Spain.

It will make you change your lakes for ocean.

## Ted

I have to conceal a lot of this for reasons that will become apparent.

Ted was a twin and spoke to his brother Brian every day. One day he couldn't get ahold of his brother, so he went on over to his house where he was met by his wife.

"Where's Brian?"

"Out with one of his whores probably."

"Karen, I don't have time for this shit. Where is he?"

"I dunno."

Ted went to the police immediately and they told him he couldn't file a report until 24 hours after he went missing. He insisted they start looking for him, to no avail.

Four days passed when the police finally got a warrant to search his house. They found Brian, cut up into pieces. Karen had tortured him before she killed him. He had burns on his body. They found ligature marks and the rope she used. She drugged him and dragged him to the basement.

There is only one women's prison in Kentucky, so drunk drivers were in the same place as murderers. Sharon, one of the women there, had killed six people and fed them to her pigs. She was doing life plus 25.

Ted reached out to her as a member of a Christian outreach program at his church.

Karen's trial began by and by. Ted's rage had no end. He wrote to Sharon in prison and told her that her pig feeding was not his business and that Jesus was her friend. He started sending her a monthly stipend for her commissary. He set up an untraceable PO box. He paid a year in advance in cash. Eventually Sharon asked Ted if they could be more than friends? Ted was more than happy to comply but explained that he could not visit her anytime soon.

Karen's trial was soon over, and she was convicted. The details of Brian's torture only focused Ted's rage. Karen was sent to the women's prison. Inmates can only have 4 transactions a month. Ted sent 4 money orders a month for $1 to Karen's account so nobody could send her more.

A few months passed as Ted and Sharon talked about marriage. Ted finally told Sharon that they could not be together because he had met another inmate who he had been corresponding with and that she would get out so they could have a future together and she could have conjugal visits. He told Sharon about his new love Karen who insisted that he no longer correspond or send money to anyone and he was sorry but this was true love.

Sharon did not take this news very well and went to talk to Karen about this. She waited until Karen was in the shower and went with a hot curling iron which she used to perforate her colon and cauterize her most sensitive area.

Karen almost died but she had a life-saving colostomy. She was in the hospital for a month. She has to walk with a cane now. Sadly, she has to be in solitary confinement because her colostomy bag makes her an easy target for abuse. It was a horrible and terrible thing that Ted told with truly infinite satisfaction.

He still sends her 4 $1 money orders every month.

### Mrs. Theiss

There was an English teacher at Oldham County high school who was supposedly a witch.

A couple of buddies of mine told me who she was when she came into eat at the restaurant we were working at. They told me all you have to do is stare at her. She was sitting at the bar waiting on a table. She was on a swivel bar stool and there were stained glass windows dividing the bar from the dining room because you could smoke at the bar then.

So I was bussing this table and I stared at her for a good ten seconds. Suddenly, she swiveled 180 degrees and looked at me. Then she winked at me. The hair on the back of my neck stood up. I went over to her.

"You're from Crestwood aren't you?" She asked me, having absolutely no way of knowing that.

"Yes ma'am I am."

"You live in that big Tudor house off 329 don't you?"

I looked at her like I had seen some manner of ghost because that's exactly where I lived.

"I remember you. You were the one who called Mrs. Theiss a stupid bitch, aren't you?"

My senior year of high school, my dad and I got into a pissing contest and he told me I was going to Oldham County High and not St. Francis. I didn't care because they had a baseball team and I was better at baseball than you can imagine.

So he enrolled me there and they put me in all the college preparatory classes. Mrs. Theiss was the English teacher. Now, I had Dean Robertson as my English teacher at St. Francis and she makes Sylvia Plath and Eleanor Roosevelt seem like Men's rights activists on the feminist's activism scale. Women in the Bible, Jane Austin, Maya Angelou, Virginia Woolf and other women authors were requisite in her class. She drove us like an angry slave master. She had an Emily Dickinson poster in her class that would later drive me to know her as intimately as one could.

St. Francis is a special school where we were encouraged to ask questions and interact with our teachers. Some kids would, some wouldn't, as you can expect. Well, you can guess how I was. This was my first day in public school and this was one of those 'the teacher lectures and you shut up' type situations, only nobody told me.

The first thing we were going to learn about was in Mrs. Theiss's class was Beowulf, which seemed appropriate because I was already sure she was a direct descendant of Grendel. Mrs. Theiss began class with "Now girls, we just have to face the facts here. There are no female heroes."

I busted out laughing so loudly that it was obnoxious. When I caught my breath, the class was silent.

"You can't be serious? I mean this is a joke, right?"

"No it is not!" she said sternly.

I pictured Dean's famous scowl which would melt and destroy egos big and small. It's simply absolute contempt and it only reared its fantastical head when someone said something incredibly stupid like when someone asked her if the past tense of "shit" was "shat." I had nightmares of that look in her eyes. So nothing about this was scaring me.

"Perhaps you'd like to enlighten us, Mr. Clay?"

"Well off the top of my head: Hester Prynne, Jayne Eyre, Rosa Parks, Joan of Arc, Harriet Tubman and Anne Frank."

I honestly do not know what came over me to start rattling those names off like that, but it was if she had insulted my dearest Dean and all that she taught me.

"Mr. Clay, I don't appreciate that kind of insolence or arrogance in my class."

It was as if time stopped at that time and the evil Thomas and angel Thomas popped up on each shoulder and we began arguing the merits. She was right, I was extremely arrogant.

Devil Thomas: "Do it! She asked for it and she deserves it."

Angel Thomas: "You've gone this far; you may has well shove a harpoon into this whale. Fuck this school."

Me: "Well fellas, looks like we're getting a GED. "

"If you weren't such a dumb bitch I wouldn't have to correct you," I shrugged.

The front three rows of girls covered their mouths like Jason Mamoa had just disrobed. If Mrs. Theiss' eyes could kill, she would have vaporized me right then and there. "Report to the principal's office immediately!"

The principal broke out laughing when I told him why I was there.

"Actually, I said she was a dumb bitch." I told the witch with a smile.

"I meant to thank you, but you left so soon after that. I remember the special ones too, Thomas."

The other guys I bussed tables with stared at me in stunned surprise as I held out my hand to her. "I have your table ready madam." She had on those elbow-length gloves on. Stood up and took my hand.

"I don't believe it's our turn is it?"

"No ma'am it isn't but I have been told by some of your former students that you are a very special lady and special ladies don't sit with loud vulgarians while I'm working."

I led her to her table, my co-worker's eyes on me the entire way.

Don't you ever tell me there are no female heroes.

## Atticus Finch

"Never let them see who you really are," my mom would say.

"Why?"

"Because they'll only try and tear you down. You have to wear a mask that pleases them. You have to talk like them. You have to act like them because you will never *be* like them."

She was always right, my mom, even when she was wrong. She'd giggle at me saying that. She was the smartest woman I ever knew except when it came to sports. We'd play trivial pursuit and I'd get all the pies but the entertainment pie and she'd get all but the sports pie. Then we'd play for hours trying to get the last pie.

I had jury duty once. I was about 20 when I was called. I was on the grand jury for about ten days. I knew the county attorney. He was a good man actually, which is especially rare for prosecutors. Prosecutors are among the most powerful people in our society and most allow that power to go to their heads.

There's a conference room in every courtroom in the country and that's where the wheels of justice grind up the people in it. My dad would take me to work so I would learn how to practice law. He once told me that law school was the greatest waste of time ever and that he literally learned nothing in law school. He learned early that a good lawyer knows the law and a great lawyer knew the judge. His father taught him that and his father and so on going back generations.

I remember this one particular prosecutor who was a real SOB. We were in the conference room and we finished just before lunch and he was putting all his cases away into his briefcase. One of the cases they disposed of was a black guy who struck a police officer. I heard his lawyer say: 'he was in the hospital for a week.'

"You want consideration for some ghetto thug who punched a police officer? You're not serious. I'll give you 18 months in county and be grateful for that because his rap sheet is as long as my arm."

"I am serious. Officer so and so seems to put a lot of people in the hospital. If you want to take it to trial then that's fine by me."

That's an empty threat and every prosecutor knows it *EXCEPT* when my dad says it. A few of them made the mistake of thinking my dad was bluffing but that is one of the admirable things about him, he would go to trial just to punish any prosecutor who thought he didn't mean what he said.

"I'll take 6 months and suspend the sentence for a year."

"I'll give you 12 months in county and 2 years' probation. Take it or leave it."

"Sold."

Everyone shuffles out of the room for lunch and the prosecutor says to me: "you gonna join the family business?"

"Maybe."

"Who's your favorite lawyer?"

"Atticus Finch."

"I don't get it."

"I didn't think you would."

I was dressed well for my grand jury duty and the others chose me as foreman. I think because the county attorney gave an anecdote about a case he had with my dad. The first case brought to us was a drunk driving case. When lawyers say a prosecutor can indict a ham sandwich, they're not far off. People generally submit to power and don't question the people trying to protect us from criminals.

The next case was a child abuse case, only this time we had a witness to testify. She was a white woman dating a black man. She gave a very teary and convincing account about her boyfriend spanking her white son for not 'minding' him and it just went "too far." He whipped the boy with a belt, and it left marks. They had pictures. Apparently, the boy had called him the N-word as well.

So we were asked to return a true bill for first degree child abuse. When we began deliberating, it didn't take long for it to get ugly. We were all white. This was in 1990. Most of the others were older.

"I don't know what she thought would happen dating a N-word."

"Bunch of savages is what they are."

"Of course he beat the white boy for calling him a N-word."

"He belongs under the jail for beating on that poor little boy."

To return a true bill, it only takes a majority vote and the majority would have lynched this guy if they could have. I signed the bill not signifying my dissent vote.

About a month later, I was looking in the paper and saw that the woman who testified was indicted for making a false police report. I went up to the courthouse about a week later to get my new license and I saw the prosecutor.

"Say what was the story about that case?"

"She made the whole thing up. Her parents disowned her for dating a black guy. That was the only way to get back in their good graces."

They dismissed the charges against him.

That's what a little racism will do. It destroys lives and does irreparable harm to others. That's why nearly half the population in every jail in this country is filled with people of color.

This has consequences for all of us, and horrible ones at that. We'll spend millions of dollars putting an innocent black person in jail, but we won't spend money on black kids to have a classroom with heat in it! And why is that you wonder? Because the evil of racism still percolates just below the surface of American society. We see it every single time a white jury acquits a white cop who murders an unarmed black person.

Do you think our black brothers and sisters don't get the message? And what do you say when they dare to complain about the injustice that breaks apart their families and communities when we so casually commit acts of liberticide against them?

Some white people like to complain about the civil war statues being taken down. You know, the ones with 'black friends.'

The first thing that must be done to eradicate the mental infirmity of racism is to recognize it. Folks just love to ignore the fact that these monuments were erected by racists and ignore the implications they dole out to blacks across the south. They were erected to intimidate blacks. These men they glorify wanted to keep them in chains for fucks sake. and they would still be in chains if not for the blood of 750,000 Americans that these traitors spilled.

Most white people do not have the mental acumen to know what dire effects their racism has. They are benefactors from a society which has cultivated white privilege while abrogating the history into some benign precept that it was about state's rights. I know this because I have spent years watching those effects play out in a courtroom in Louisville and they are pure evil.

Even a tacit acceptance of racism has dire consequences in a jury room or in a ballot box. That is why there is so much injustice in this country, because of the fine woke folks who are glad to proclaim: "I'm not a racist. I have a black friend." But when they get in the jury room, 400 years of white privilege come oozing to the surface because racism is marrow-deep in them.

So don't expect me or anyone of conscience to be polite to such people. I will do whatever I can to stem the flow of racism wherever I see it and vehemently protest against any purveyor of it. And I'll be damned before I sit by and let your quiet racism destroy the lives of our black brothers and sisters who have bled just as much for this country as anyone else!

Martin Luther King Jr. said: "He who passively accepts evil is as much involved in it as he who helps to perpetrate it. He who accepts evil without protesting against it is really cooperating with it."

If that's the world you want, then you are the very antithesis of an American and I want nothing to do with your ignorance and hatred.

## Brother Tim

Jimmy Carter exemplifies the kind of Christians my grandparents were.

It's one thing to preach or testify to your faith but it's quite another to live it. The pastor used to come down to my Pop's shop and whatever we were doing, he stopped what he was doing, and we'd go fix a lawn mower or change the oil, it didn't matter.

It took years of this kind of thing before my exhaustion from religion turned to contempt. If you focus your education on the members of the Greek Academy where Plato and Aristotle once walked, and do a careful reading of those giants, you couldn't allow faith to survive because faith is the opposite of reason. That was the impression of my youth.

Today, I know that faith is the enemy of reason.

My grandmother once told me to never discuss religion or politics if you want to have a civilized conversation. She never told me why. I guess her plan was to let me learn that the reason in good time, which I did. I can count on fingers and toes how many times I've been to church. Call it opposition research if you like.

When my mom got cancer, they gave her three months to live. Two years after that, we had gotten doing chemo into a routine. She'd sleep. I'd read until my eyes hurt as I tried to keep my focus away from those god-awful soap operas that were always on. The kids ward was just across the hall. In a cancer ward, you always feel like one endless wave of impending doom. It was dreary on a good day. Playing with the kids was a way to escape that feeling. Mom would do chemo for 5 days, once a month.

This particular day, I was playing with Katie, a sweet little freckle-faced girl with High-risk Medulloblastoma , when I see my grandparents walk in with Brother Tim. He was one of these pastors who would come interrupt Pop and me whenever it suited him. I knew he was there for some prayer. So there I am talking to Katie and we're playing Uno when she says, "I'm not going to make it." You can imagine how that made me feel.

I lied to her and said I had to go talk to the doctor about something and hugged her before I fucking lost it. I wanted to cry. I wanted to stab something. I would have murdered a million people to make her better.

I walked in on Brother Tim preaching to my mom. She asked him why god gave her cancer.

"Cancer is god's punishment for sin."

My mind exploded with rage. If I had anything to kill that bastard in my hand I would have. I did so much worse.

So in a calm and restrained voice, I said, "So tell me Tim, what did those kids over there do? What's their sin?"

"They're paying for the sins of their parents."

"So your god punishes children for the sins of their parents?"

"That's right."

"Then your god is a sadist."

Me saying "your god" broke my Granny's heart. She gave me a look of contempt that still hurts me. When I said god was a sadist, she never spoke to me like her grandson again.

When people are alone and in their comfort zone, they will show you who they are. If you really want to know someone, start talking religion with them. You don't have to prod an evangelical to talk about religion. They naturally want to convert you.

In high school, I had a Christian missionary who was my Spanish teacher. She was a beautiful woman, too. On Saturdays, a church in St. Matthews allowed the Hispanics to hold services in Spanish, so she thought it would be a good experience for me to come to church with her. She didn't have to ask me twice.

I was better than conversational in Spanish then and I was the teacher's pet to be sure and I was more than happy to enjoy looking at so grand a female specimen. She said they were Baptist Dominionists. I hadn't heard of that one before.

When we walked into the service, I realized my hormones had gotten the better of me. The Pastor comes up and we make pleasant introductions and my teacher said it was my first time in church. It wasn't. It was the first time in THEIR church. That meant that I needed to get baptized and saved because my immortal soul was in great peril.

"Are you ready to accept Jesus Christ as your lord and savior?"

If you remember Bill Murray in the movie Ed Wood when he was being baptized so they could make a movie and the pastor asks him in the swimming pool if he accepted Jesus as his savior and he goes: "Sure," that was me.

So he takes me by the hand and drizzled water on my head and praise the Lawd, I was done saved. I was then part of a club that I had no intention of joining.

After all the pomp and circumstance, we had lunch in their cafeteria. That's when the pastor started hitting me with the 'god's law is the supreme law' and that they were hoping for the battle of Armageddon to begin so Jesus would show up to rapture all the believers up to heaven and the best way for them to accomplish this was to arm Israel so they could start a holy war against the Palestinians and bring the second coming.

This was a tad overwhelming but then I remembered why my Grandmother Clay told me to never talk religion. Right then and there I finally understood the gravitas of what she meant.

I remember a shift in the evangelicals in the early 80s. What changed was cable came out. Jerry Falwell, Pat Robertson, Jim Bakker and their ilk stopped preaching the virtues of Jesus Christ and began preaching hatred. Falwell was 'the moral majority' who were a sect who damned anyone who was gay. What ALL these pastors learned from Oral Roberts, Falwell and the purveyors of hate was that hate was much easier to sell and infinitely more profitable.

The result of that hate for homosexuals was nothing short of a holocaust and they had a complicit enabler in the White House named Ronald Reagan. They all thought this was divine punishment from god who was punishing them for their mockery. Of course we could spend trillions on defense and space lasers but only a couple of million on HIV prevention. I remember so many Christians saying they prayed for every f\*\*got to get AIDS.

The largest megachurch in Kentucky is Southeast Christian. My in-laws were congregants and they were determined to cure me of my atheism. I didn't mock their faith, but I wanted to, badly. So they invited me to come to their monstrosity of a church. It was obscene. They spent over $100 million on this church. They had a large daycare service. They had copper gutters. Most of all they had a huge following that required multiple services on Sunday.

My wife told me I only had to do it this once, so I did. They had a band which played a song, Until the Rapture. It was catchy, if you're a Christian I guess. This particular service was about fornication and it took all I had to not laugh out loud at their amazing hypocrisy.

I kept replaying that Until the Rapture tune and I was finally able to say out loud 'they're no longer a religion, they're a death cult.'

Do you want to know why Republicans don't care about the environment? To answer that you have to understand that there are two kinds of Republicans. The stealers and believers. The stealers only want to exploit the religious zealots' vote so they can loot the environment for profit. They don't believe in climate change because to believe it would mean regulations to control companies who profit from its exploitation. The happiest countries are also the most regulated.

The believers don't care about the environment because Jesus can come down whenever and cleanse the oceans and clear out all the greenhouse gases with a wave of his magic wand. They're going to heaven anyway so who cares if there's no more whales? Who cares if Israel is exterminating

Palestinians? That's what they want. They want Jesus back as soon as possible and the costs be damned.

That is the harm of Christianity these days because the haters stifle the voices of real Christians. This is why people are leaving religion in droves and that's a good thing because these megachurches want to destroy everything for future generations because they *ALL* say we are living in the end times according to the Book of Revelation.

We have a bunch of Dominionists in our government who think biblical law supersedes constitutional law and they mean to put as many Dominionists as they can in seats of inscrutable power while progressives and liberals quibble about who gave speeches and who is a neoliberal while losing races, all the livelong June.

The only thing that matters is winning and that's why these stealers and believers will lie, cheat and steal every election they can because they do not make the mistake of splitting their vote on candidates who only run every presidential cycle.

Know your enemy and stop treating them as friends because they mean to do you harm. We have to fight just as dirty as they do because 'when they go low, we go high' didn't work out so well.

We need to talk about politics and religion endlessly because a well-educated populace is something that terrifies evildoers and oligarchs alike.

Resistance must be active and provocative.

Otherwise this republic will go the way of the dodo.

## David

My mom was an artist.

She was brought up in the Southern Baptist church and my how they bred contempt in her. We had a garage apartment that she rented out and there was this madman named David that lived there for a while. He was a Navy SEAL. Yeah, yeah, I know. No really, he was. He had all these pictures of himself in Grenada when Ronnie Reagan decided to invade.

I haven't thought about this in 20 years, but he took me on a pot run one time. David was always armed with a pistol and at least two knives. So he goes into this house and buys his weed and comes out and fires up a bowl expecting to have something of quality, but it was Mexican stick weed. So he goes back up to the house, opens the screen door and kicks the door in. I didn't see what happened but believe me I was good and scared. A few minutes later he comes out carrying a garbage bag. I could not get over the look of calm on his face because I was certain something bad was happening. He threw the bag in the trunk and got in.

"I'm good on weed for at least 6 months."

He told me when we got home that he tied up the pot dealer and then called up the dealer's mom to come untie him. Told her that her son was a thieving bitch and if he ever tried robbing anyone again, he would get really angry. David was fucking batshit crazy. He could do things I did not know were physically possible. He was never just still, and he smoked more pot than any human alive.

But the best thing about David was that he had every issue of Playboy there ever was.

One day David just up and left. Never saw him again. I walked in the apartment and back into the bedroom closet and there they were. A note said, "they're yours bud."

Box after box of Playboys.

I carried the loot up to my bedroom knowing that my collection was better than my dad's and I set about memorizing every damn one of them. Terry Welles and Candace Collins were my favorites. It didn't even occur to me to ask my mom permission to hang the centerfolds on my wall. I just did it. My friends would visit as if they were in Mecca. I remember filling in all those nail holes 25 years later thinking what a pain in the ass it was. Jeff Spicoli could kiss the entirety of my ass though. I had ALL OF THEM.

Hugh Hefner is gone now, and the world is poorer for it. Depending whether you're a critic or fan, he was either a great man or a real bastard. History will tell. Personally, I am going with the real bastard end of the spectrum because teaching boys to objectify women has led to more horror than we can fathom but can we blame him for unintended consequences? He loved women in his own way, and he bled that into me. Every straight man wanted to be him, including myself.

## Donnie

Our 'justice' system has nothing to do with justice.

It is a revenue stream where our government extorts money from the poor in exchange for their liberty. And it's extremely profitable, too. Right now in states across the country, you can buy as much cannabis as you like and the police can't do anything about it, while in states like Kentucky, you can get a year or more in jail for an ounce of weed.

Nobody should be in jail for weed. Nobody.

One of the things that is kept secret from the public is how much it costs to try, convict and imprison someone for an offense. I was in jail with a guy named Donnie Ray in Boyle county, Kentucky. He got snagged into a sting operation between local police and the DEA. It was called operation November Rain.

The way it worked was that the local police turned prostitutes they had arrested into informants. They were given a deal - help us arrest 'dealers' and you can walk out of here, but you have to wear a wire and catch us some 'dealers.' Since most of these women were addicts and did not want to go through withdrawal in jail, they were all too eager to take the deal.

One of them went to see Donnie. Donnie was an opioid addict and this girl went to buy two hydrocodone pills. His nickname was 2pills in jail. Donnie was guilty as he could be. He fessed up immediately: "There weren't no point in denying it." He was arrested, arraigned and awaiting sentencing. In the interim, he lost his job. His ex-wife had to get on welfare to help pay for their two kids. Donnie had to have oral surgery to remove three teeth because in jail, the only choice you have is to pull teeth. Fillings don't happen.

Those two pills he sold to an informant cost less than $5.

The thing is that the federal government pays grants to states who enforce drug laws. The last I looked about 9 years ago, it cost $43,000 per year to house an inmate per year in Kentucky. Donnie got sentenced to two years. So for $5 in pills, the taxpayers paid out $86,000 plus however much it cost in welfare benefits for two kids.

The police and DEA arrested 86 people in that operation. If just half had a similar outcome, then we're talking millions of dollars for one single county.

There are 750,000 immigration cases pending before the immigration tribunal courts, which is a department in the Justice Department. There are 350 judges to handle 750k cases. That's 2,140 cases per judge.

At the 'Tender Care' detention centers, we are paying $2,000 a day to house toddlers in a private prison company. We are spending $800 a day to house their parents. Take a wild guess who they contribute campaign money to? This is for misdemeanor offenses.

Meanwhile, our teachers are working extra jobs to make ends meet and our infrastructure is falling apart because we as a people would rather spend $86,000 on $5 worth of pills than elect responsible stewards to office who will check this evil prison industrial complex which has bought off every crooked Republican in congress pointing their sleek fingers at the refugees fleeing a drug war that *we* started.

The fiscal irresponsibility of Republicans will impact generations of unborn Americans to come. We are doing lasting and irreparable damage to these children just so the private prison lobby can make a lot of money.

Something to remember in November.

## I.Q.

Let me tell you something about growing up in the South. Racism is so ingrained in the culture that it is marrow deep.

I know, I was exposed to this kind of shit in my youth and I was certainly racist before I knew anything. It was bled into me and it took a conscious and concerted effort to rid myself of the affliction.

The first airplane I ever got on was Piedmont Air on a trip to Chattanooga. I was going to visit Baylor, which is an old military boarding school my dad went to. His English teacher, Mr. Hitt picked me up at the airport and as soon as we got in his car, he began to give me a lecture on the history of Martin Luther Ni**er. I remember him going out of his way to tell any 'boy' he saw to do something when we were on campus.

I've been to a few college campuses: UVA, Berea, Hanover, Vanderbilt, Stanford, Haavad, but the most beautiful of all is West Point. I'd venture to say that it is some of the best real estate in the world. It's high on a hill overlooking the

Hudson river. The buildings are made of thick stone and it's just stunning in every way except inside the buildings.

But as stunning as it is there, Baylor is more beautiful. The tuition there in 1984 was $20,000 a year. Kentucky is the south; Tennessee is the deep south which is just code for more racist and hoo doggy! was it ever. I don't know if Mr. Hitt was actually in the Klan but he was an authority on 'Martin Luther Ni\*\*er.' He was a white-haired product of the deep south.

One of my favorite movies as a teen was The Lords of Discipline because my dad wanted me to go to West Point like you would not believe. It's about some college kids coming of age when they finally allowed a 'goddamn ni\*\*er' to come into their military school. The black student was portrayed by Mark Breland who later won a gold medal in boxing. It's a damn good flick.

In the movie he is subjected to torture by a secret society of students called The Ten who were supposedly the ten best Cadets at VMI and that was a real group, I later learned. VMI trained most of the officer corps in the Confederacy and VMI was and likely still is a white supremacist institution. It's the only college outside of the military academies that you can earn a commission in the military from.

We are all products of our environment and I too am a product of that same 'Southern Heritage' you hear from those intellectual eunuchs who froth at the mouth whenever the statutes of traitors are toppled and who chant, 'Jews will not replace us.' My dad is a lawyer. In my formative years, I would go to work with him and though I did not have the wisdom to raise my voice in protest to what I witnessed, I do now and with more life experience, the angrier I've become because as Machiavelli said, 'A true patriot hates injustice in his own land more than anything.'

It took me 43 years to flee my Old Kentucky Home when that same corrupt justice system put me in jail for a crime I did not commit. I can flatly state from first-hand knowledge that the police are corrupt, the prosecutors are corrupt and so are the judges. There are a whole host of reasons, but the root of corruption is racism, pure and simple. It is not something I will ever be silent about or complicit in ever again.

Hate is a terrible thing to teach kids.

One night in Louisville Kentucky, there was a football game between Ballard High School and Central. Ballard is in the east end of Louisville which is the more affluent part of Jefferson County. Central is in Downtown Louisville and it's mostly black kids there. The game was at Ballard and those kids were passing a watermelon through the stands. I shouldn't have to mention how unspeakably ugly and disrespectful this was to the black kids. What is more infuriating to me is that none of the parents there or coaches who saw this did anything to make this a teachable moment. That absolute failure as human beings is why their football program should be cancelled entirely.

Passing this mental infirmity onto your children is child abuse, plain and simple. The parents of these children are teaching their children that this bullying and degradation is acceptable, as well as the school administration. This isn't kids having fun. This is why in almost every jail in this country, half the inmate population is composed of people of color.

Is that okay with you? Because it sure as shit isn't okay with me.

This is *our* problem. Only we can cure this sickness, and it only thrives when good people remain silent about it. Oppression in all its disgusting forms is evil and if you don't stand up for what's just and right, you are human garbage and in desperate need of some soul-searching so you can stop being part of the problem.

## Jail Tale

When I got out of jail, I weighed 158 pounds.

I should probably explain why I was there in the first place.

We've heard the story a million times... boy has evil sister who's a psychopathic criminal, boy catches her robbing their senile grandmother blind, sister files a false police report against boy who ends up in jail and gets all his teeth knocked out by another inmate while sister sells off every family heirloom she can get her hands on.

Meals in jail are provided by a company called Aramark that Dumas would have made famous had they existed about the time he was writing the Count of Monte Cristo. I don't like talking about it because I still have PTSD from it. I can remember every day clearly. What we were served, I dare not call it food. It was a form of basic sustenance that a starving dog would not eat, and I am not being hyperbolic at all.

They starve you on purpose because the same company runs the commissary inside the jail. Ramen noodles that are 10 cents at Walmart are 65 cents in jail. A candy bar that was 3/1.00 were a $1.25 each last I looked. I can't bear to look at either in the store because when I do, I get a flash of synesthesia that brings back all the horror of that evil place at 6th and Jefferson. When I say that the Chateau D'If had absolutely nothing on the Louisville Metro Department of Corrections, I mean exactly that.

The whole scheme is to furnish the prison industrial complex with rich sources of revenue. If you were forced to eat something a starving dog wouldn't eat, you'd get on the phone with your loved ones and have them put money in your account so you could eat. Which brings me to the other absolutely corrupt business, Securus. They are the service that charges $1.75 for a 15-minute local call. It's $12.99 for a 15 minute out of area code call. They are moving towards video calls which are $3 a minute.

All of this is a tax on poor people who can't afford bond and it stresses already desperate people who lose their jobs while in custody, lose their housing while in custody and lose their belongings. I had a very nice Lexus SC 400 that was impounded and sold when I was in jail. I was not notified. If a car is on the impound lot longer than 3 weeks, they can sell it at auction.

Guess who gets the money? The police retirement fund.

Hunger is a weapon that jails use to control inmates. You misbehave, you don't eat. You don't have trash in the trash can, you don't eat. You have Kool Aid in a coke bottle that you bought in the commissary? You don't eat. These are all violations that can get you sent to the hole and while you are being transferred to the hole, you don't eat. One time they were bringing this guy from the hole back to general population and it was right after lunch trays had been served, so he didn't eat. But it was commissary delivery day which is once a week. So this little guy had a "big sack" and this guy waits until the guards are gone, and he goes and takes the little guy's candy bars. He tries to fight back so this guy starts beating him into unconsciousness. The guards eventually come and carry the guy out while saying he's faking. He was in intensive care for several days at $15,000 a day. So you and everyone else who pays taxes paid over $100,000 so Aramark could sell a hungry inmate a candy bar for $1.50 that cost them .30. The little guy that was in jail was charged with misdemeanor shoplifting.

Say you wanted to be a good Samaritan and help the guy that was getting beaten. Well you better be Bruce Lee because you will get beaten worse for the crime of "meddling" and everyone else will help beat you. It is quite literally social Darwinism at its worst.

I couldn't eat that shit. After a couple of weeks of seeing man's inhumanity to man, I didn't want to endure it. I stopped eating for 23 days. I gave my trays away for Kool Aid. I was in the worst opioid and Benzo withdrawals that you can imagine. I was pissing blood from kidney stones. I didn't care if I died. I wanted to be out of that most terrible place. I was in with this Marine who had done three tours in Iraq. He came back and started with alcohol and moved to meth. He told me about war and seeing what happened when his buddies hit an IED. He had this tattoo on his arm that covered a grotesque scar that said GAISLICK or something like that for Global Artillery School or something. He said, "I'd much rather be in the shit than be here. At least there you eat good and you don't have to fight for toilet paper." The guards love to play petty games because on the outside, they are $15 an hour high school graduate nothings. Inside, they are gods and they make sure to let everyone know it.

I was beat up by some fucker with a cast on his arm. I only remember the first hit upside my head. I was in intensive care for 9 days and the hospital for 11. Lost all but three teeth. It was another reason why I was in such despair. I thought if I got sick enough, my dad would get me out.

He didn't.

When I finally got out, there was an Arby's just down the street, so I got a beef n cheddar and curly fries. I'll never eat at Arby's again as long as I live. It doesn't take even a month to become institutionalized. I was afraid to go out. I was afraid to go to the store but when you are starved on purpose and for profit, when you get out, you want to eat like a hog, and I did. When I stepped on a scale it said 158. I was normally between 191 and 205. When I quit smoking, I gained almost 50 pounds.

It took a while to get my head straight and to put that shit behind me. When you're poor, you can't afford decent food so it's easy to gain weight. Eventually, I took Andy Dufresne's advice to 'get busy living or get busy dying.' I am so far away from Louisville now that I can finally breathe. Tonight I bench pressed my own weight, 220 pounds. Never doubt your ability to change. William Blake said, "a man who does not alter his opinions is like standing water and breeds reptiles of the mind."

Believe me when I say, I've killed crocodiles you can't imagine.

## Ron

I was a Republican once.

Or at least I thought I was. In high school, that is. I wanted to be like my dad like any son. He just loved Ronald Reagan. He kicked those commies' ass. He knocked down the Berlin wall. Kids these days didn't have to practice ducking under desks in case there was a nuclear attack from Russia. The collapse of the Soviet Union to my young mind was like popping a big zit, just complete relief.

In my underclassman years at St. Francis, there was one teacher we had who stirred terror in all of us. He had an unbelievably loud and booming voice. Sometimes he screamed and yelled at someone so loudly that other teachers would have to close their doors. Sometimes they'd scoff and roll their eyes and simply say, 'Mikulak is at it again.'

It was known to all that Ron had a bit of a temper and he *might* have had what some will remember as a "short fuse." If anyone had to grade where Ron was on the political spectrum, well, let's just say between Ronald Reagan and Karl Marx, Ron would say that Marx was a fascist. Which was odd because he ran his classroom so stringently that he would have made Stalin blush while quipping, 'I've got nothing on this guy.' I liked him instantly.

If he thought all that hootin' and hollerin' impressed me he was in for a rude awakening because unbeknownst to Mr. Mikulak, my dad was an International Grand Champion of screaming and yelling. *Everyone* called him Mr. Mikulak lest they raise his wrath. So of course I called him Ron. He had an old Mondale campaign sign in the window by his desk.

"Hey Ron, how'd that Mondale vote turn out for you?"

For those of you who have never witnessed a conniption fit in person, allow me to explain. First the sufferer freezes as if to say, 'did he just say what I think he said?' When the shock and awe begin to take hold in an anger junkie, sparks begin to churn like Ixion's grindstone which invariably ignites the fuse to a thermonuclear rage bomb that's about to detonate in their brain, which powers up the hate-beams that come blazing out of their eyes like Superman's. Imagine the alien bursting out of Window's skull in the movie The Thing. That will give you some idea of the Rage-Beast I had just unleashed.

Ron smoked a pipe and I remember the sensation of his rage-spittle landing on my face. "Do you think I was going to squander my vote on that vacuous empty-headed ignoramus?!!!!!"

I don't know if anyone else lost a significant percentage of their hearing that day, but I sure as hell did.

I only needed Ron's class and a sports elective to graduate. Our single biggest project was what we called The Melancholy Dane Society. We spent an entire semester reading Hamlet aloud in class. It was intense and Ron guided us through every nuance in that masterpiece, line by line.

Then my mom died. This toxic patriarchal society killed my best friend and it did it slowly.

I didn't much care about school or anything then. Inside, the worst depression took hold. I went long enough to turn in my Melancholy Dane Society paper. I turned in something on the ghost and it was crap. I didn't care. Mom had surgery to remove the tumor, then she was doing the harshest chemo and radiation there was. Radiation was the worst. She would barf at anything.

I missed 63 days my second semester. I was trying to keep my mom alive.

I went in for my final exams and I had not even looked at whatever I was supposed to read during second semester. I think it was Othello. I opened that exam and knew nothing. I just started writing a letter to Ron. I explained what was going on and that I was sorry I didn't come to class. I told him I would try and make up for it.

A few weeks later I got my grades from St. Francis. I didn't open them for several days. I knew I had failed. I hadn't failed at anything before. I would have to do a stint in summer school or something. When I finally got the courage to open it, I saw his distinct writing and a C- on it. He passed me. It was the first kindness I had felt in what seemed forever from a man who I thought would never show it because he was hard and he demanded excellence.

He shattered every illusion I had of what reading National Review said liberals were. As the tears streamed down my face at his kindness, I swore I would be worthy of that C-. That C- changed me more profoundly than words can express.

That was the day my education really began.

Education is lethal to republicanism. Truth cures sophistry, and compassion can lead someone out of the darkness. That's what this man taught me. He is the best teacher I ever had. I cannot repay the debt I owe him. I can only pass on the gift he gave me.

## Jeopardy

I will never beat my dad in Jeopardy.

Dad only reads books about WWII. His book shelf had maybe 60 odd books when I started reading proficiently at 11 or 12. I did like to read, but the reason I wanted to read those books was because trivia and jeopardy were blood sports in my family and I thought if I read all the books he read, I could play jeopardy as well as he could. The Rise and Fall of the Third Reich was one of the first. The Last Lion was next. I felt pretty smart then about my WWII knowledge because I was just a kid.

When I read a book, it becomes part of me. My favorite book about WWII is Inside the Third Reich by Albert Speer. It made me realize how little I knew, and I understood my dad's fascination with the subject, and it kept me reading even more. There are sub-genres like Dunkirk, D-Day, the Battle of the Bulge and so on. It's almost impossible to be fluent in all of them but dad has pretty well mastered the European theater and has been doing the Pacific theater for maybe 20 years. Last I saw his bookshelf, it had maybe 300-400 books on it.

I was fool enough to think that fiction didn't matter because it wouldn't help me beat my dad in Jeopardy. If I had a child now, I would make sure they only read literature. It develops your mind so much more.

One of the things I learned from the 2000 election is that those of us who have studied history are doomed to watch it repeat itself. Oscar Wilde studied history too. He said:" All empires fall, there are no exceptions." We are an imperialist country. We morphed into that because conservative chicken hawks made us this way. They've never much liked diplomacy except when they need it to build another military base. More bases mean more influence. If other countries don't want freedom then by God, we'll deliver it to them, even if we have to commit atrocities to do so.

I used to wonder late at night, why didn't anyone do something to stop the Nazis from doing what they did? It takes years more of studying the first world war to really understand it. There are so many terrible lessons to learn from war. One of them was that there was a lot of profit in war. You cripple a nation financially and you'll make a very devoted enemy.

Alexander the Great and Napoleon learned this lesson rather rudely. Then you always have the revisionists distorting history to conceal the atrocities their homeland commits when they go to war.

The Red Orchestra was a group of dissidents in the Weimar Republic led by a man named Harro Schulze-Boysen. Red Orchestra helped Jews escape and were generally involved in undermining everything Nazis did. They were called 'communists' because of the 'red' in their name, but they hated Stalin as much as they hated Hitler.

Harro was just 33 when he was caught by the Gestapo. He wrote a letter to his parents before his execution called the 'this death suits me' letter. It's worth reading.

I am completely calm and ask that you accept this with composure. Such important things are at stake today all over the world that one extinguished life does not matter very much... everything that I did was done in accordance with my head, my heart, my convictions, and in this light you, my parents, must assume the best... It is usual in Europe for spiritual seeds to be sown with blood. Perhaps we were simply a few fools, but when the end is this near, one perhaps has the right to a bit of completely personal historical illusion."

During the 30s, the Nazis slowly eroded the public's confidence in their established institutions. They used propaganda to poison the minds of the people they meant to rule. It took the right economic conditions and nine years of work before Hitler had what he needed to complete Germany's descent into fascism. The descent into fascism has taken almost 40 years for Republicans. Evangelicals are naturally fond of authoritarianism because it matches their faith that there's an old white man living in the sky who wants to take care of you if you just praise him and give him money.

Republicans don't need concentration camps. They simply control how much money you have. Money equals freedom and as much as they bray about how much they love freedom; they sure don't want anyone to have the freedom to see a doctor or the freedom to move to other places. That's why Republicans will never vote to increase the minimum wage because it was such a spectacular success when Johnson implemented it. Gutting the middle class is essential to their future plans and they are doing extremely well in handing over more money to the rich people they serve. It's easier to manipulate people who are in financial distress.

If you want to see a man's real character, give them power. I have said many times that *ALL* Republicans are liars and I damn well meant it. They are also the most disgusting hypocrites the world has ever known. They are ignorant and stupid. I can make the same aspersions against the people who voted in the Weimar Republic. They made a deal with the worst devil ever known and rather than admit it and correct their mistake, they doubled down.

The world paid an unthinkable price for their short-sightedness and stupidity.

## Lesli

My sister has a very broad foot.

She's four years older than I am and when I got big enough to hold a crayon and scribble outside the lines, she took me into our dining room to teach me how to write my own name. It was 1974, I was four. Dad was a Captain in the Army then, on his way to becoming a lawyer. Mom was an art teacher. I always wondered how oil and water could fall in love and have children but so it was and soon not to be. Lesli sat me down and started showing me on a tablet of tracing paper how to write my name.

The first real trouble I had ever been in was when I was sent to the principal's office in kindergarten. I didn't even know I had done anything. I got sent home with a sternly worded note. Mom was telling me that I was in big trouble when dad got home. Even at four I knew I had committed a major felony and a beating was sure to follow. I could only wait in nervous anticipation by flexing my cheeks in anticipation. I thought about stuffing my pants with a shirt or some sort of unknown body armor but it would have been futile. Dad drove a 911 T and to this day the sound of that engine gives me panic attacks and did with each successive model.

Mom was waiting at the back door as dad came in. She handed him the note, "See what junior did?" I knew when she called me junior that we had gone past the major felony into a federal offense.

"Dear Mr. and Mrs. Clay, your son called Michael a "Fucker" in front of the whole class," my dad read.

"Who the fuck did he learn that from?"

"I wonder," replied my Mom.

It was as if the dark clouds of a beating began to form and just as dad passed me, I squinted and waited for it and I heard him climbing the stairs. Then the skies parted as relief overcome me.

After teaching me how to write my name, I proudly went to show my mom what I had done. I was watching Walter Cronkite talk about the Watergate break in when I learned that it took a sister to commit a federal offense.

"What the fuck is this shit?" Dad was never one to mince words. I turned to look and saw him coming at me like a heat seeking missile. Lesli had generously and kindly used the tracing paper to write my name in crayon all over the dining room walls. My ass was on fire for several days, maybe a month. My memory is still a bit hazy after that beating.

She loved her records and listened to them endlessly. I was 12 or 13 when I learned what real pain is. I foolishly borrowed her Blizzard of Oz record. I had forgotten to return it because adolescent boys have the attention span of a gnat. She bypassed opening the door to my room and kicked it in instead. She thunder-footed over to my turntable as I got up to apologize and plead for mercy.

"Don't ever come in my room again," she screamed at the top of her lungs as she did her best Bruce Lee kick to my groin. Her foot was wide enough to get everything of importance. That was the first time I ever felt real pain. I was certain my life was coming to a very sad end. I imagined my tombstone saying, 'here lays Thomas, kicked in the nads so hard by his sister that he keeled over.' The pain comes in waves of intensive agony and it would soon become the favorite sport of all my sisters.

That somewhat describes the sensation I had in the wee hours of November 9th, 2016.

## Mary

I grew up with 3 sisters and a mother. I was always outnumbered.

If I disrespected women, I paid dearly for it. "Oh Thomas, we all have been through that." Oh REEEEEEAAAAALLLY? Have you now? Let me tell you about the last time I left the seat up.

I was 16. I had my own bathroom, which was connected with our guest bedroom, but I was the only one who used it. I had just bought a $700 waterbed which was totes cool and awesome. I was a busboy and saved up the money to get it. So I'm fast asleep dreaming about swimming, or so I thought. I felt a bit of wetness and woke up suddenly to the coven of sisters standing by my bed and Cathy holding a utility blade. She had slit my waterbed open.

"Now you know how it feels fucker!"

I knew better than to protest. This was justice, I guess.

If you have known ten women in your life, then you have likely known a victim of rape or sexual abuse. If she cared about you, she might have told you what it did to her. I've known several. What has always struck me is the soul crushing pain a rapist inflicts. I hate them.

If I were benevolent dictator for a day, I'd make rape a capital offense and I would let the victim decide whether they get life in prison or death. There are no "accidental" rapes. It's about consent.

Casanova was once asked what the greatest aphrodisiac was? He said, "A woman, wanting to be enjoyed."

My sister Lesli is four years older than me. She had two BFFs, Leah and Mary. Mary had long brown hair all the way down past her butt. She was maybe 5"1" and she was one of those women who developed young and her assets were impossible to miss. She was also extremely beautiful.

She was my first real crush.

My mom was extremely libertine about everything so long as we were at her house. And that house was a huge two story eight-bedroom Tudor. For Lesli's 17th birthday, she wanted to have a party and apparently, she invited everyone at Oldham

County High School. She bought a pony keg of Busch lite, the worst beer ever made. There were several bottles of bourbon, a bottle of peach schnapps, a bottle of Rumple Minze peppermint schnapps and a bottle of Tia Maria.

It was a Saturday night when everyone showed up. There were at least 75 people there. We had a poker game going in the dining room. I won a real Stetson hat off some guy and a switchblade off another. I kept wandering around watching everything and making sure nobody stole anything. There was a lot of pot, too.

In the kitchen I saw the girls playing drinking games with beer and peach schnapps. Mary had this ridiculous laugh that could drown out the sound of 75 loud and intoxicated people. She was just a tiny thing. Before long she was sitting on some guy's lap who had no idea the murderous rage I was trying to channel through my angry stare. I noticed that she had gotten up and fallen back into the lap of this dude and he grabbed her gloriously large round supple breast as she landed.

I considered whether to go get my machete or just use an ax to kill him for touching the future Mrs. Clay. I settled on an ax before I realized that Mary had way too much to drink. So before I decapitated this miscreant, I needed to get Mary out of the way so we could get married and make babies later. I scooped her up and carried her upstairs to the guest bedroom next to mine. I almost dropped her trying to climb the steps with all these people on it. I laid her on the bed and covered her up. There was one of those red dome lights in that room, so I turned that on in case she needed to find the bathroom. When I switched it on, I looked back and she was out.

I wanted to go back and play poker but by this time there was a waiting list. So I poured a Busch and tried to act like I was a grown up. Ate some chips and dip and I heard some guy ask where "Tits" was? It looked like there was going to be a double decapitation this evening if these fuckers tried to touch my crush.

I got back to the stairway and I looked up and I saw these two guys whispering. Then one walked out of view towards Mary. As I came up the steps, I heard the door lock click. The way our house was laid out, there was a bedroom and a bathroom between the next bedroom. The bathroom door couldn't be locked because mom didn't install it correctly.

I knew what was happening.

Mom had bought me a 12-gauge single-barrel shotgun for my 12th birthday. I went in my bedroom, into my closet, loaded it and pushed the bathroom door open to find this fucker Jeff on top of Mary and trying to lift her shirt up. I put that shotgun 2 inches from his forehead and cocked the hammer. REO Speedwagon's "keep on loving you" was playing loudly from downstairs.

I looked at him with murderous eyes, "Not on my watch, fucker."

I am positive his life flashed before him. He knew he was caught.

I thought about shooting him, but I loaded a rock salt round and knew it wouldn't kill him.

"Please" he said feebly.

"It's time for you to get the fuck out of my house."

I didn't have to say it again.

I was raised by three sisters and a mom. Mom was molested when she was a girl. When I told mom what happened, she hugged me and said, "that's my boy."

To this day, I still put the seat down.

## Maybe

'Sticks and stones can break my bones but words will never hurt me.'

Don't teach your kids that. It's bullshit. Words kill. Let me tell you about the power of words. We burned Japan to the ground. Every city in Japan was ash except two. We left Hiroshima and Nagasaki alone because we wanted to see what the bombs would do to them. The War Department decided the bombs would be used, and they planned on using them, but it was Truman's decision. It was the most important decision in world history until that moment. He told Clarke Clifford that if he didn't use it, what would he say to the mothers of all the sons who were going to die invading Japan? Acheson hated the decision.

These were perhaps the best staff the US ever had. The truth was that Japan was whipped and Truman said so aloud and wondered why they wouldn't surrender. They thought their emperor was a god and god would deliver them victory. Captain Tibbets set off to prove to the Japanese that he was not a god. The damage assessments were worse than the best scientists the world had ever known estimated. Hiroshima was leveled in a firestorm that has not been seen since. We awaited Japan's surrender. Truman went on television and told the world and the Japanese specifically that we had more of these bombs and would use them to terminate this war.

That was August 6th, 1945. No word came from the Japanese on the 7th.

On the afternoon of the 8th, the Japanese sent word that "maybe" they will surrender. There is no word for 'maybe' in Japanese. It was a translation from Japanese into English. Truman got this message and was enraged. He wanted full and unconditional surrender not maybe. He ordered Nagasaki bombed. What was lost in translation was that Japan agreed to surrender. That 'maybe' cost 80,000 people their lives. Think about that when you say that words don't matter.

## Mrs. Whitney

I wish a Vulcan mind probe were possible.

It may happen one day. A brain implant which transfers information is within the realm of possibility. Imagine being able to download all of the knowledge one mind has. I think it will happen one day. Imagine if we still had the entire contents of the Library at Alexandria!

I have a book clicker in my brain which keeps count of the books I've read. The first book I got was from my Grandmother Clay. It was a Fred Flintstone picture book. It was maybe 4 inches by 4 inches with 128 pages and if you flipped them, there was Fred doing a dance on the top right corner. I don't remember learning to read. My mom would read to me and I would follow her finger on the page.

I remember my first day of 1st grade at Emmitt Field Elementary School in Crescent Hill. I walked into Miss Whitney's class and why it was remarkable was because she was black. The only black person I knew was my father's nanny, Addie. I walked up to her and asked: "Can you make chocolate cake like Addie?" This was apparently hysterical to her.

"I make pretty good cake, sugar." She had this book on her desk.

"Can I read this?"

"I don't know. Kenya? It's in Africa. May I is correct, sugar."

"May I read this?"

"You know how to read already?"

"Yes ma'am."

"Then you may borrow it."

I went home and read it straight through. I brought it back the next day. My mom was an art teacher. Before we moved to Oldham County, mom took my Kindergarten, 1st and 2nd grade teachers out to lunch to thank them and talk shop. Mom was one of the leaders of the '76 strike at the board of education.

Our house had a library in it and there were maybe 8-9 thousand books in it. After mom died, I had to pack up the books because two people in that monstrosity of a house was too much and the utilities were around $600 a month. I found this book in it. I opened it up and saw 'Property of Emmet Field Elementary'.

There was an inscription: "To Thomas, never stop reading. You are a very smart boy." Mrs. Whitney.

Well Mrs. Whitney, I just turned 4992 on my book meter just short of my 48th birthday. I've learned so much since I read about the sneezing horse. Mostly I've learned how tragically ignorant I will be because a lifetime isn't enough to grow past a few disciplines.

The majority of my books were history books. American history was my focus for a few years. Now I am only interested in literature. I'm about to get fluent in Sci-Fi. Maya Angelou said: "when you get, give and when you learn, teach."

I've always believed that knowledge is power. It has fueled my desire to learn. The better minds I have read have several characteristics in common. "Question everything" is their common refrain. Plato, Aristotle, Dante Alighieri, Spinoza, Wittgenstein, Turing, Dostoevsky and many more.

There's part of me that wants to teach because when you get done with a good book, you want to go tell others about it and share what you learned so others can be in on the secret.

The thing is that you can only teach those who want to learn, and that's a lot harder than you might think. And some who want to teach, really don't know how to. I had a teacher in middle school who told my dad I was "retarded." Fortunately, I had teachers in high school who repaired the damage that ignoramus did. I read more. I learned more because no hick was going to define me.

The right books coupled with the right teachers can open dimensions for you.

I'm very grateful for the ones I've had, the ones I have, and the ones to come.

## Peregrines

Archimedes was the greatest mathematician of antiquity.

He set forth much of the foundation of applied mathematics without so much as a pencil to work with. His powers of concentration were legendary. When Roman soldiers came to capture him from his home in Syracuse, he answered the soldier: "Noli, obsecro, istum disturbare." Don't disturb that sand - meaning the sand on which Archimedes was working out a problem. The soldier, feeling disrespected no doubt, killed him.

Now think, for a moment of the hands that took the life of Archimedes. The hands of an ignorant soldier, a man who had no chance of understanding what was in front of him, or the importance of Archimedes' contribution. Likewise the hands that ground the hemlock of Socrates, cut the throat of Cicero, drove the nails of Jesus Christ, or pulled the trigger on two Kennedys and Dr. King.

Never forget that your intelligence and your willingness to do good is no defense from ignorant brutality. Stupid people are dangerous, especially in groups. If you would not be a victim (a martyr is a victim who got a consolation prize once they were safely dead) then prepare and watch the brutes.

## Monsters Among Us

I loved my friend Kirk like a brother.

We grew up together in a very small Kentucky town where there were ten times as many churches of varying denominations as there were schools. My sister, being the proverbial "fag hag" in high school was friendly with all the gay kids. Kirk was one of those kids and that is how we met.

Regularly, our gay friends were sent to this 'pray away the gay' camp which is euphemistically called 'reparative therapy" that was about 100 miles from where we lived by their evangelical parents, who lied to them about where they were going.

Many others weren't as lucky.

It was a hot Saturday night in 1986. I had just gotten my license a couple of days before when the phone rang. I could hear my Mom's voice, "What? What happened? WHAT! Where are you? I am on my way."

"You drive, Thomas," she barked at me. I used to race motorcycles and was driving on the highway since I was old enough to touch the pedals on my Pop's truck. She didn't like to drive so fast like she did in the days when she and dad lived on a base in Germany, where I was born, and drove on the Autobahn.

It was raining that night too, like a heavy monsoon rain.

We left as soon as Kirk called, around 11 p.m. He was the guy every girl in high school lusted after. Imagine a 6'2" dark, Italian Adonis and as Queer-Eye-For-The-Straight-Guy gay as you can imagine. Many, many women tried to "cure him" of his gayness, but to no avail. He would often say: "I'm a terminal fag, Thomas." I'd respond:, "But Kirk you can have any woman you want!" He would scoff in utter disgust.

Whenever I was arguing with him about something, I'd run to get my sister's tampons and throw them at him. I think Kirk would have preferred I threw cat shit at him. Women repelled him as much as men did me so that was the basis of our friendship. I did man stuff and he did gay stuff which made mom endlessly happy.

It was a different time, when gay people were subjected to unimaginable cruelty, hate, physical abuse, and levels of homophobia that we cannot even fathom today. At least, not in this country and not today. But it remains the same in many places around the world.

Mom and I drove through the night and the rain got so hard that it was like trying to drive through a kiddie pool at 50 mph. By the time we got to Versailles – pronounced 'Ver–sales' in Kentucky – it began to let up. I was pushing Mom's Honda Civic to its max speed of 85mph. The lightning and thunder were awe-inspiring, and I had learned to have a serious respect for Mother Nature after living through a deadly tornado a few years before.

I rounded a curve as the most vicious lightning struck across the sky and the thunder sounded like an atomic explosion. Up in the distance, something came up from the side of the road. A tall, lanky biped in a white tee-shirt and underwear with its arms raised in the air flailing furiously. It was Kirk.

Blasphemy seemed apropos as I stopped the car.

"Jesus Fucking Christ."

He collapsed into our welcome arms — not just sobbing, but bawling his eyes out the whole way home as he told us of the torture he had endured the last couple of days. Please understand that I do not use the word 'torture' lightly. That's what these "good Christians" had done to him. Torture. Whipping, beating, starving, isolation.

Imagine 30 teenage "terminally gay" kids out in the most rural part of Kentucky in a fenced-in camp. Such a place needs to be private so they could ply their disgusting trade. Mornings were devoted to first scripture class where hellfire and damnation were imminent if these abominable sinners did not repent their evil ways and turn their lives to Jesus. Then more Bible study about, 'man shall not lie with a man as he lies with a woman.' Lunch was a bologna and cheese sandwich. Sinners do not eat breakfast for what I later learned was a $5,000 "reparative therapy" course.

That's what the parents paid to have their gay children tortured.

That was the carrot, to make them see the error of their ways and if they had just sworn to repent and be saved again, they wouldn't get the stick. Some did, some didn't. Most were intimately familiar with 'spare the rod, spoil the child.' Fridays were for the rod. If you wouldn't pray the gay out of yourself, they would beat it out of you.

I saw the bruises on Kirk's back when he peeled his shirt off. His back was black and blue from the bottom of his shoulder blade down to his knees. He said they used a wooden stick and took turns screaming and beating him. "Are you going to stop sucking dicks faggot?" was their favorite taunt.

We got him home. Something was different, the twinkle was beaten out of him as he discovered man's inhumanity to man. He got in the shower until the hot water ran out. He was safe now. When he got out, we fed him. I remember how he was before and how he was after. I don't want to say that he was broken because he wasn't. All that ugliness takes a toll on any human being. I remember praying that night and saying aloud: "forgive them, Lord, for they know not what they do."

We made that trip at least another 30 times over the course of several years. We reported them to the police on multiple occasions. They said that it was a "Christian school" and that, "beating faggots" was not illegal. Those 'good Christians' made me into an atheist.

Kirk went back home, only to have his parents send him back to the Pray Away the Gay camp after they lied to him and told him they wouldn't. It's okay to lie to a person whose soul is in jeopardy of damnation if you're a Christian. I think he wanted to go back so he could save some of the others. He told us later that he carved a message under one of the bunk beds with our number on it.

He didn't stay long this time. He grabbed one of the others, Craig, and tried to escape but they were caught by the staff. You can imagine what they did to Kirk and Craig. Thursday night and all day Friday, they were subjected to the 'reparative therapy' of being beaten with a stick. They waited until 2am on Saturday to make their break. It was damn near 3 am when the call came. Mom came in and told me, 'we've got to go get Kirk again.' I had a young man's seething rage boiling my blood. I drove as fast as I could through the night, determined to kill every one of those bastards if I could.

They were maybe three miles closer than before. That's how far they had walked through the night. They were so scared that the people at the camp would catch them. When we got there, they told us there were cops searching for them. Craig had a black eye and a busted mouth. He fought back, brave little bastard. Craig was "a woman trapped in a man's body." He had long blonde hair and blue eyes. Transsexuals always had it worse, I was told.

Craig stayed with us for a few days. He cleaned endlessly so my mom told him he was welcome to stay as long as he wanted. I remember him calling his parents all week in what seemed like an endless negotiation.

And I remember the blood-curdling scream, the wailing that rips your soul apart, when Craig's mom called Kirk to tell him that Craig had hanged himself.

CPSIA information can be obtained
at www.ICGtesting.com
Printed in the USA
FSHW012350100120
65834FS